Becoming God's Last Days Anointed Warrior

Workbook Series
Volume One
Keep What is Written

Lessons On

1. America - a Former Christian Nation
2. Warnings for the American Church
3. Seals - Horsemen - Martyrdom
4. Opening the 6th Seal - A Great War is Coming
5. God's End-Time Warriors 144,000

A study guide in conjunction with
lectures and video lessons by

DR. DONALD BELL
MAJOR USMC RET.

Becoming God's Last Days Anointed Warrior
Workbook Series Volume One: *Keep What is Written*

July 2019
Copyright © Dr. Don Bell

All rights reserved. Printed in the United States of America. No part of this publication may be reproduced, stored in a retrieval system, or transmitted, in any form or by any means electronic, mechanical, photocopying, recording, or otherwise, without the prior written permission of the author.

Scripture taken from the Holy Bible, New International Version®, NIV®. Copyright © 1973, 1984, 201 Biblica, Inc.™ Used by permission of Zondervan. All rights reserved worldwide. www.zondervan.com The "NIV" and "New International Version" are trademarks registered in the United States Patent and Trademark Office by Biblica, Inc.™ All rights reserved.

Scripture quotations are from the Holy Bible, English Standard Version® (ESV®), copyright © 2001 by Crossway, a publishing ministry of Good Publishers. Used by permission. All rights reserved.

Scripture quotations taken from the New American Standard Bible®, Copyright © 1960, 1962, 1963, 1968, 1971, 1972, 1975, 1977, 1995 by Lockman Foundation, Used by permission. (www.lockman.org)

Because of the dynamic nature of the Internet, any web address or links contained in this book may have changed since publication and my no longer be valid. The views expressed in this work are solely those of the author and do not necessarily reflect the views of the publisher, and the publisher hereby disclaims any responsibility for them.

ISBN 978-1-943412-05-1

Published by -
Wilderness Voice Publishing, LLC
Canon City, Colorado USA
www.mcgmin.com

"A voice crying in the wilderness - proclaiming the good news of the coming Kingdom!"

Table of Content

Session One: America a Former Christian Nation — 4

Session Two: Warnings for the American Church — 26

Session Three: Seals, Horsemen, and Martyrdom — 53

Session Four: Opening the 6th Seal: A Great War is Coming — 76

Session Five: God's End-Time Warriors "144,000" — 94

Ministry and Resource Information — 114

"AMERICA"
------ ------ ------
A FORMER CHRISTIAN NATION

SESSION #1 – WORKBOOK
Intended For
"KINGDOM WARRIORS IN THE ARMY OF GOD"

Unveiling Mysteries in the "Book of Revelation"

Based upon the Book:
GOD'S ANOINTED WARRIORS
By
Dr. Donald Bell
Major USMC, Ret.

(Slides # 1 - 5)

AMERICA – A NATION FOUNDED ON CHRISTIAN VALUES

Key Points:

- Godly leaders founded this country under the biblical principles of justice, truth, and religious freedom. America is the first and only country in the New Testament age founded upon Christian values.

- Our present-day heritage of freedom, peace, and prosperity is the fruit of our forefathers' obedience to and love for, the Lord Jesus Christ and His heavenly Father.

- The Lord obviously has called America as the most powerful representative in the world of Christianity under the new covenant and over the last 400 years, it has evolved to be the most influential nation in the promotion of Christianity throughout the world.

- Over the last four centuries, she has greatly influenced most of the nations of the world with the gospel truths of Jesus Christ.

- Additionally, thousands of patriotic Americans have died on the battlefields around the world fighting for our freedoms that we enjoy today.

(Slides # 6 - 11)

COMBAT PRIORITIES FOR MARINE CORPS OFFICERS

Key Points:

- 1st – Our Assigned Mission

- 2nd – Lives of Men in our Unit

- 3rd – Our Own Life is to be Placed Last

Notes – How does this apply to you?

_____
_____
_____
_____

BREAK-TIME   (Slides # 12 - 13)

(Slides # 14 - 16)

AMERICA – A NATION GONE TERRIBLY ASTRAY

<u>Today, we are a country:</u>

➢ Where prayer and Bible study are no longer permitted in our schools. Although our college campuses are floating in New Age & Islamic teachings.

➢ Where the presence of our Lord is not welcome in governmental facilities. Even military chaplains are being warned not to pray in the name of Jesus. However, again Islamic and New Age-style religions are quietly being embraced.

➢ Where the American news media has brainwashed many of our citizens into embracing corrupt government agendas leading to a major disregarding of our constitutional freedoms.

➢ Where abortion clinics have butchered tens of millions of babies over the last 35 years and now our tax dollars fund abortion clinics across the world. This child sacrifice has been made lawful in order to support sexual immorality resulting in the continuing slaughter of young, innocent victims. Planned Parenthood clinics have been secretly selling body parts taken from these unborn children.

➢ Where violent and demonic television, movies, video games, coupled with widespread drugs has spawned a dangerous belief system within our youth culture. <u>So many of our youth of today are "technology smart" but "life stupid."</u>

➢ 21st century America is now a country that embraces a "godless" lifestyle that has given rise to a dangerous drug-influenced American culture that welcomes adultery, abortion, pornography, homosexuality, and same-sex marriages as a normal way of life.

➢ A country that was founded on biblical principles established by almighty God has now chosen to throw off our Christian heritage and embrace the principles of Sodom and Gomorrah.

Sadly, our nation no longer worships the Lord who blessed us with prosperity and established our religious freedoms. For we are a nation that needs to listen to the following warning:
➢ *Woe to those who call evil good and good evil, who put darkness for light and light for darkness, who put bitter for sweet and sweet for bitter!* **Isaiah 5:20**

_____
_____
_____

(Slide # 17)

OUR CURRENT ADMINISTRATION

I do Believe

- That our current president, together with those he appointed in high governmental positions, are truly committed to our constitutional and religious freedoms which have been foundational to our country.

- However, this sudden and surprising emergence of a conservative, republican administration has brought about a visible division between patriotic Americans and those venomous and hate-filled anti-Americans - who are committed to destroying our heritage.

- However, my friends, I do believe that our Lord has initiated this sequence of events in order to visibly reveal to His church - that we are no longer the United States of America – we are now the Divided States of America and this division is rapidly and visibly escalating all across nation.

- So do not allow this current patriotic surge with the election of President Trump and his administrative successes to date, lull you to sleep. America has crossed the line – a very destructive and challenging time lies shortly before us.

(Slides # 18 - 19)

NATION WILL RISE AGAINST NATION

Ethnos will Rise Against Ethnos

➢ A hate-filled division has suddenly emerged within America and this is one of the signs that Jesus said would occur prior to His 2nd coming. **That is, in Matthew 24, Jesus said that in the last days, "nation will rise against nation."**

➢ In the original biblical language, the word for "nation" is "ethnos." Thus, it should be interpreted that in the last days "ethnic groups will arise against ethnic groups."

➢ This is so visible in today's America where our constitutional freedoms have allowed "hate" to emerge among different ethnic groups.

➢ We are a country where racism is rampant – where the liberal hatred toward conservatives is horrific – where our President is treated like an enemy among numerous American peoples.

➢ Now this sudden division is not just a difference of opinion – it is a hatred to all those who disagree with one's beliefs.

(Slide # 20)

During Our Lifetime:

➢ If we put our hope in government – it will fail!

➢ If we put our hope in man – it will fail!

➢ If we put our hope in the Lord Jesus – it will never fail!

➢ We are called to be very watchful and continually seek the Lord during these times, for Jesus Himself warned us that "a nation divided against itself cannot stand." This has been historically true with numerous nations such as ancient Israel and the Roman Empire.

Christian warriors – "stand fast." Dark times are rapidly approaching.

_____
_____
_____

BREAK-TIME   **(Slides # 21 - 22)**

(Slides # 23 - 26)

WORLDLY INVASION OF THE AMERICAN CHURCH

<u>The Kingdom of God – The Church:</u>

➢ Represented by a tremendously huge, marble-like boulder (pearl) reflecting a gloriously beautiful light much greater than the sun and emanating an overwhelming sense of holiness.

<u>The Kingdom of the World:</u>

➢ Represented by a black, octopus-like demon with tentacles that were progressively blackening the light and consuming the holiness of the Lord's church.

Why isn't the American church standing stronger against this ungodly, worldly invasion of our beloved country?"

➢ The church of this present is under attack from the worldly kingdom which is replacing much of the true gospel message with subtle lies.

➢ The deceived worldly church will soon join with the worldly government in their war against the remnant of Christians who will not compromise their faith.

➢ A pure light will be powerfully released into the darkness in the midst of disastrous times that lie before us.

Notes:
_____
_____
_____
_____
_____
_____
_____
_____
_____

(Slide # 27)

MULTITUDES OF FALSE TEACHERS WILL ARISE IN THE "LATTER DAYS"

Beware –

For the time is coming when people will not endure sound teaching, but having itching ears they will accumulate for themselves teachers to suit their own passions, and will turn away from listening to the truth and wander off into myths. **2 Timothy 4:3-4**

Key Points:

➢ This is how numerous modern-day liberal heresies have subtlety crept into the world of American Christianity

➢ They are deceived teachers who will twist scripture with the objective of building a base of followers who they will unknowingly lead astray

➢ This is effective because the majority of Christians are biblically ignorant

➢ They are prone to believe the teachings of some supposed man of God because they are charismatic speakers who tickle people's ears

➢ In the days of Jeremiah, false teachers among the Jews continued to preach peace and prosperity and insist that the love of God would never allow them to be invaded by the heathen Babylonians.

➢ The people listened to these comforting teachings and continued on their merry way, buying and selling until, suddenly, terrible destruction fell upon them and destroyed them as a nation.

Notes:

(Slides # 28 - 29)

RAMPANT IN AMERICA:
BIBLICAL TRUTHS REPLACED BY LIES

So many pulpits have become virtually silent on the most powerful life-changing truths of the gospel.

Key Points:

These are churches that embrace the philosophy of "humanism" which teaches that the end of all things is the "happiness of man" rather than the "glory of God."

➢ Lukewarm Churches avoid the Preaching of the Cross

➢ Christian welfare mentality – provides feel-good teachings that perpetuate self-absorption & empowers the ego of the listeners

➢ Christians are misled to jump into a resurrected life by a shortcut that bypasses the continuing work of the Cross in the believer's life

➢ The teaching that Christ did everything for us & we don't have to suffer death to our carnal self is a deadly doctrine which leads to the wrong destiny

➢ Worldview are crying out "Make love, not war"

➢ Their definition of "love" is far different than biblical "love." It embraces a lifestyle of "tolerance which is a modern-day doctrine of "political correctness."

Notes:

(Slide # 30)

THE PREACHING OF "TOLERANCE" IS FROM THE ENEMY

Key Points:

➢ "Tolerance" is a doctrine that effectively weakens the truth of the biblical gospel.

➢ "Tolerance" doctrines assume man is basically good even though they may need periodic counseling help

➢ "Tolerance" is currently being communicated worldwide by non-believers as the ultimate expression of "true love"

➢ Eventually it will become unlawful to share the truths of the biblical gospel because that would be considered "intolerant"

➢ The time is coming when Christians that proclaim that Jesus Christ is the one & only way to eternal life will be maligned as extremists & unloving fanatics who are a hindrance to the establishment of a peaceful society.

The world-view voices in our nation today are getting louder and louder crying out "Make love, not war!"

➢ These world-view voices continually speak about living a happy and successful life, but in reality, they conceal the truth that leads to true eternal happiness.

Notes – Consider how "tolerance" is being communicated in your environment:

_____
_____
_____
_____
_____
_____
_____
_____

(Slides # 31 - 32)

WORLDVIEW VOICES IN AMERICA
CONCEAL BIBLICAL TRUTHS

Key Points:

Why do they conceal the Truth?
- They love to embrace worldly pleasures & do not want to hear that their chosen lifestyle is leading down a dark, sinful road.

- They want to believe that man is "basically good" and can choose to live their lives without interference from God.

- They do not want to hear the truths of the gospel that reveals them to be "sinners" destined for eternal darkness.

- They do not want to hear that Jesus is the only way to eternal life. They want to believe that all roads lead to a joyful afterlife.

- They do not want to believe that their worldly lifestyle is hated by God.

Jesus Warns Us – Do Not Love the World!

Do not love the world or the things in the world. If anyone loves the world, the love of the Father is not in him. For all that is in the world— the desires of the flesh and the desires of the eyes and pride in possessions—is not from the Father but is from the world. **1 John 2:15-16**

Characteristics of the Worldly Social System in the "Last Days"

But understand this, that in the last days there will come times of difficulty. For people will be: *Lovers of self - lovers of money – proud – arrogant – abusive - disobedient to their parents – ungrateful – unholy – heartless – unappeasable – slanderous - without self-control – brutal - not loving good - treacherous - reckless, - swollen with conceit - lovers of pleasure rather than lovers of God –* ***Having the appearance of godliness, but denying its power. Avoid such people. 2 Timothy 3:1-5***

- In other words, they may profess to be Christians but refuse to give up their worldly lifestyle.

_____
_____
_____
_____

BREAK-TIME (Slides # 33 - 34)

(Slides # 35 - 36)

WHAT OUR MISSION "IS NOT"

Key Points:

Soldiers in the Army of God need to understand that:
➢ We are not forces of revolution attempting to establish a righteous government in this present world.

This world is not our home:
➢ Until it is finally liberated, it belongs to the Enemy. In fact, soldiers in God's army are despised by the world.

John 15:19
➢ *If you were of the world, the world would love you as its own; but because you are not of the world, but I chose you out of the world, therefore the world hates you.*

➢ Those who are consumed with desires of the flesh & worldly possessions hate God the Father and His Son Jesus Christ who calls them out of the world.

Our army is probably better characterized as guerillas behind enemy lines with a mission to proclaim the true gospel message of Jesus Christ, as the Son of God, to those currently in the world.

(Slide # 37)

WHAT OUR MISSION "IS"

Key Points:

Our assigned mission is to lead those held in captivity to the world:

1. Out of the darkness into the light.
2. Out of deception & into the truth
3. Out of an evil lifestyle into righteousness
4. From eternal damnation & misery into eternal life & joy

The kingdom of God, led by our Lord will never betray His soldiers fighting to free others.

Jesus Christ will continually encourage and strengthen us to **"make war, because we love."**

(Slide # 38)

MISSION DIFFERENCES:
WORLD'S SOLDIERS & GOD'S SOLDIERS

Key Points:

Soldiers of the World may die carrying out their mission to:

- Kill their Enemy or
- Take Prisoners Captive

Soldiers in the Army of God may also die carrying out their mission to:

- Love their Enemy &
- Free Prisoners from Captivity

Questions to personally consider:
- How do you respond to Christian brothers who want to revolt against the government?
- How would you respond to American militia forces that come to take away your property?
- Is the use of firearms proper? In what situations? (I address this in a handout entitled "Physical Preparations"

Notes:

(Slide # 39)

JESUS CHRIST – HIS LEADERSHIP PRIORITIES

Most Christians are not aware that the true meaning of <u>hosts</u> in both Hebrew and Greek is **"a gathering army organized for war."**

<u>Key Points:</u>

<u>**"Hosts" = A Gathering Army Organized for War**</u>

In contrast to the liberal world-view voices who cry **"Make love, Not war"**

Jesus Christ, our true Commander-in-Chief calls us to: **"Make War because We Love"**

<u>Priorities taught Marine Corps Officers:</u>

1. Mission Assigned by our Commanders
2. Lives of those under our authority
3. We were to place our own life last

<u>Priorities of Jesus Christ – Our true Commander-in-Chief:</u>

1. Assigned Missions = Will of His Father
2. Lives of all who choose to follow Him
3. He placed His own life last to provide salvation for all who follow Him in order that His chosen people among mankind will live eternally with Him

---

<u>**Also the two greatest commandments of our Lord are similar to these leadership priorities:**</u>

1. We are called to love the Lord with all of our heart, soul, mind and strength. God is our primary focus on the battlefield of life. Love Him before all else.
2. We are called to prioritize others before ourselves with a heart of true love.

Notes:
_____
_____
_____
_____
_____

(Slides # 40 - 41)

CHRISTIAN WARRIORS IN THE ARMY OF GOD

The Great Warriors Of The Bible

- Always went through periods of darkness before they were brought into the purposes of God.

- The purpose of the wilderness journey is to conform us more & more into the image of Jesus Christ and to bring us to a place of maturity where He can trust us with more authority.

- Remember warriors, there is no victory without a battle. We must see every test as a great opportunity and no matter how dark it seems to get, the light will surely dawn, just as the sun comes up in the morning.

The Whole History Of The Church Is - The Arena Of God Versus Satan In Trials By Ordeal:

- As you see on the screen, Satan's champions will always be more numerous and will visibly appear to be greater and more powerful since they are supported by worldly governments and pagan religions.

- It hasn't changed; but it is about to get more challenging than ever before.

- Yet, warrior-spirited Christians standing uncompromisingly for our Lord will always prevail in the strength of the Lord.

- The praying believer will never faint during hard times. On the contrary, he will grow stronger and stronger – because he trusts in God before he trusts in men.

Christian Warriors need to memorize the following verse in Isaiah 40:29-31

He gives power to the faint, and to him who has no might he increases strength. Even youths shall faint and be weary, and young men shall fall exhausted; but they who <u>wait</u> for the Lord shall renew their strength; they shall mount up with wings like eagles; they shall run and not be weary; they shall walk and not faint.

- In other words – continually seek His face and develop that personal one-on-one relationship with Jesus and your heavenly Father.

_____
_____
_____

BREAK-TIME (Slides # 42 - 43)

(Slides # 44 - 45)

MISSION FOR THE "BOOK OF REVELATION"

The Book of Revelation provides us with detailed information concerning events that will take place prior to the Lord's return to setup the Kingdom of God on this earth.

Our Lord promises great blessings to those who **read, hear** and **keep** the prophetic messages communicated in the Book of Revelation.

Listen to His words at both at the beginning and at the end of this Book:

***Blessed** is the one who **reads** aloud the words of this prophecy, and **blessed** are those who **hear**, and who **keep** what is written in it, for the time is near.* **Revelation 1:3**

*"And behold, I am coming soon. **Blessed** is the one who **keeps** the words of the prophecy of this book."* **Revelation 22:7**

The Book of Revelation together with other prophetic books is intended to provide Warrior-Spirited Christians with:

➢ **Understanding** – of the times & purposes for these events.

➢ **Direction** – for our ministerial calling in the midst of these events.

➢ **Preparation** – to "be ready" both spiritually & physically.

➢ **Encouragement** – to be <u>a glorious light</u> within our respective environments during these times.

We cannot continue to ignore or downplay these prophetic events any longer.

Notes:
_____
_____
_____
_____

(Slide # 46)

THE BOOK OF REVELATION
MUST REMAIN OPEN TO BOTH KINGDOMS

IT MUST BE COMMUNICATED BY THE CHURCH IN THE MIDST OF CATASTROPHIC EVENTS.

The result will be twofold:

- For the people of God, it will strengthen their faith as they look beyond the tribulations to the coming of the Lord Jesus.

However, there will be many who want nothing to do with it:

- They will mock and belittle those who proclaim it calling them hate-filled pessimists who are scaring people.

- It will arouse opposition from unbelievers who's hope lies within the world.

- Those who proclaim end-times prophecies will one day be considered a threat to national security and the world's agenda.

Let the evildoer still do evil, and the filthy still be filthy, and the righteous still do right, and the holy still be holy. **Revelation 22:11**

Consider how you will handle the Book of Revelation! Teach? Listen? Obey?

Consider your calling during these "last days"

Notes:
_____
_____
_____
_____
_____
_____
_____
_____

(Slides # 47 - 48)

REMAIN STEADFAST IN THE FOLLOWING TRUTHS

1. God speaks to His people in this life through both the Old & New Testaments.

- The Bible is God's revelation of Who He Is and Who We Are together with the relationship that exists between God and man.
- The Scriptures are not man's witness that God exists, but God's witness to man.
- The Bible was written by men who have been chosen by God.
- However, these men are not the authors of the bible – God is the true author for he breathes His words into the hearts of His chosen writers.
- Thus, the words in the bible are true in every respect.
- And it is through these very words received from our Lord that His people are to understand the following truths which He revealed to us.
- <u>That is:</u>

2. Jesus Christ is God's Son who came to earth to pay the penalty of death for all those who believe on His Name.

3. Mankind is a natural born sinner who cannot enter the kingdom of God unless this sin has been washed away by the shed blood of Jesus Christ.

4. Jesus Christ is the one and only way to eternal salvation. There is no other way.

5. One must be truly "born again" in order to enter the kingdom of God. These are those who repent of their sins and render obedience by walking in the truths of God.

6. No one born of God makes a practice of sinning for God abides in him and he in God.

7. Jesus Christ is truly divine and existed from all eternity as the Son of God. He is the Word of God that was present when creation was spoken into being.

Notes:
_____
_____
_____
_____
_____
_____
_____

(Slides # 49 - 50)

THE PURPOSE FOR THESE SESSIONS

1. <u>To provide insight</u> into the tribulation events which precede the 2nd coming of our Lord Jesus Christ to establish His kingdom on earth.

2. <u>To assist our understanding</u> of the Lord's purposes for releasing devastation throughout the earth.

3. <u>To provide understanding</u> for our missional calling as Christian warriors in the midst of tremendous worldwide chaos.

4. <u>To provide some ideas</u> for equipping ourselves along with our families and friends so that we will be ready. Being ready will eliminate "fear" when the suddenness of these calamities strike our nation and other parts of the world.

5. <u>To provide encouragement</u> that you are not alone, for our Lord is raising up many others who are to be a shining light in the midst of great darkness.

WARRIOR-SPIRITED CHRISTIANS IN THE ARMY OF GOD

<u>Key Points:</u>

These are Men & Women who "Deeply Desire"-

- To make a glorious impact within the kingdom of God during their short life span upon this earth.

- To be a strong light in the midst of deep darkness.

- To make a positive impact in the lives of both believers and unbelievers in the midst of tremendous chaos.

- To play a visible role in the strengthening and growth of God's kingdom during a time of tribulation

- To hear our Lord Jesus Christ say, "Well done, good and faithful servant" when they enter into His presence.

- When that occurs, these Christian warriors will know that their calling in this life has been completely fulfilled. <u>Well done!</u>

(Slide # 51)

JESUS PRAYING TO HIS FATHER

Prior To His Crucifixion, Jesus Prayed To His Father For All Of Those Among Mankind <u>Who Choose To Follow Him.</u>

<u>This prayer is in JOHN 17:15-23 where He says to His Father:</u>

➢ I do not ask that you take them out of the world, but that you keep them from the evil one.

➢ They are not of the world, just as I am not of the world. Sanctify them in the truth; your word is truth.

➢ As you sent me into the world, so I have sent them into the world. And for their sake I consecrate myself, that they also may be sanctified in truth.

➢ "I do not ask for these only, but also for those who will believe in me through their word, that they may all be one, just as you, Father, are in me, and I in you, that they also may be in us, so that the world may believe that you have sent me.

➢ The glory that you have given me I have given to them, that they may be one even as we are one, I in them and you in me, that they may become perfectly one, so that the world may know that you sent me and loved them even as you loved me.

<u>Boy – this so unbelievably overwhelming.</u>

Notes:

LEADERSHIP PRIORITIES IN THE KINGDOM OF GOD

Key Points:

- **1ˢᵗ** – We fight for the glory of His wondrous Name in the midst of a world of darkness.

- **2ⁿᵈ** – We fight for the salvation of those in bondage to the enemy. Family, friends, co-workers and strangers that our Lord brings into our lives.

- **3ʳᵈ** – We fight without fear for ourselves for we are called to let go of this life and not be concerned for the consequences that may befall us.

For the time may be shortly before us when we hear the following calling from our Lord:

Arise, shine, for your <u>light</u> has come, and the glory of the Lord has risen upon you. For behold, <u>darkness</u> shall cover the earth, and thick <u>darkness</u> the peoples; <u>but the Lord will arise upon you, and his glory will be seen upon you.</u> Isaiah 60:1-2

Mission Objective –
Calling for Warrior-Spirited Christians to network with one-another to stand and confront the challenges that await our generation.

Notes:

(Slide # 53)

THE NEXT SESSION:

WARNINGS FOR THE AMERICAN CHURCH

First: Read Revelation 2 & 3

- Overview of Jesus' letters to the Churches

- The Church of Ephesus/Smyrna/Sardis/Philadelphia/Laodicea – do they exist in 21st century America?

- Pre-Tribulation Rapture – "The Truth is Left Behind"

- Pre-Tribulation Rapture – Christians "Wake Up!"

- Pre-Tribulation Rapture – A Marine's Point of View

- Three "People Groups" that Emerge during times of Warfare

- Three "Church Groups" that Emerge during times of Warfare

- Betrayal arises from within the Church

- Who are the "Weeds" that have been Sown in the Midst of the Churches?

- A great falling away from the church will occur in the "Last Days" – who are those who may "fall away."

Additional Notes:
_____
_____
_____
_____
_____
_____

THE LAMB OF GOD - OUR TRUE "COMMANDER-IN-CHIEF"

The days are rapidly approaching when a tremendous separation will take place among mankind.

Yet, during this present era of warfare, He reigns as our Commander-in-Chief and His Name continues to be the battle cry for those warriors who fight daily for righteousness and truth.

His name is Jesus, Our Lord, Our King, Our Commander-in-Chief

- A truly mighty Leader who would never delegate assignments to His people that He Himself wouldn't readily embrace.

- A Commander that Christian warriors will readily follow not matter the danger or what costs have to be paid.

- These are warriors whose deepest desire is to hear Jesus welcome them with the following words when they enter into His presence:

……… 'Well done, good and faithful servant. You have been faithful over a little; I will set you over much. Enter into the joy of your master.' *Matthew 25:21*

WARNINGS FOR THE AMERICAN CHURCH

(Revelation 2 & 3)

SESSION #2 – WORKBOOK
Intended For
"KINGDOM WARRIORS IN THE ARMY OF GOD"

Unveiling Mysteries in the "Book of Revelation"

Based upon the Book:
GOD'S ANOINTED WARRIORS
By
Dr. Donald Bell
Major USMC, Ret.

(Slides # 1 - 5)

JESUS APPEARS BEFORE JOHN ON ISLAND OF PATMOS

Revelation 1:18-19

- *When I saw him, I fell at his feet as though dead.*

- *But he laid his right hand on me, saying, "Fear not, I am the first and the last, and the living one. I died, and behold I am alive forevermore, and I have the keys of Death and Hades.*

- *Write therefore the things that you have seen, those that are and those that are to take place after this.*

Thus, the Book of Revelation was launched, and the first command given to John was to write the words of Jesus to seven churches located in Asia Minor which are recorded in chapters 2 & 3.

(Slide # 6)

THE LETTERS OF JESUS TO THE CHURCH

It is important to understand that these letters from Jesus to the church in Asia Minor were also meant for the entire Christian Church from the 1st century until the present day.

- Jesus speaks of spiritual ailments concerning sin which have continually weakened the Christian churches over the last 2,000 years.

- Christian soldiers need to stand back and take an unbiased and truthful look at the American church today; hopefully they will see that Jesus is not only speaking to the churches in His day, ----

He is also speaking to us.

Notes:
_____
_____
_____

(Slides # 7 - 10)

THE CHURCH OF EPHESUS --- DOES IT EXIST IN AMERICA?
(Revelation 2:1-7)

Key Points:

Verses 2 & 3 appears to indicate that the Ephesian church:

- Strong in doctrine - Faithful in Discipline
- Obviously Intellectual - Dedicated to the Scriptures
- They certainly <u>baptized</u>, <u>fasted</u>, <u>paid tithes</u>, and <u>kept the Sabbath</u> which, in their minds, was evidence of their spirituality.

BUT:
These initial accolades from Jesus are followed by a "**but**", which tells us that we are **about to hear what really is on Jesus' mind.**

BUT - They had left their first love

- Doctrinal purity and their legalistic approach to the scriptures had become more important than developing their intimacy with their Lord.

- Such routine priorities as whether the <u>services were faithfully attended</u>, the <u>sacraments were properly applied</u>, the <u>church-bulletins were read</u>, the <u>budget was paid</u>; all questions that pertained to the external life and activities of the church was its primary focus.

Consider the Ephesian Style Churches in America:

- These are churches and seminaries that possess a spirit of independence and the worship of their respective denominations exceeds their love for the Lord.

- This is very prevalent in the western world today and yet, these churches have **no idea of their lack of readiness** for the coming Day of the Lord.

Very subtly, the Christian Church can become like the Pharisees who prided themselves in their hard work and doctrinal purity.

This is a church that needs to pay attention to the following warning given by Jesus:

For I tell you, unless your righteousness exceeds that of the scribes and Pharisees, you will never enter the kingdom of heaven. **Matthew 5:20**

Notes:

Consider the Ephesian - Style Churches in America:

➢ These churches are very prevalent in the western world today and yet, these churches have **no idea of their lack of readiness** for the coming Day of the Lord.

_____
_____
_____

When Persecution Threatens these Churches:

➢ When this type of church is confronted with persecution from a worldly government, **many will not have the spiritual strength to stand against it** and many will undoubtedly compromise the Gospel message in order to maintain their status within the new governmental system.

_____
_____
_____
_____

An Eternal Perspective for these Churches:

➢ Their lack of spiritual commitment is so serious to the Lord, that He tells the church that <u>**unless they repent and return to their first love, He will remove them from their place.**</u>

_____
_____
_____
_____
_____
_____
_____

(Slides # 11 - 14)

THE CHURCH OF SMYRNA --- DOES IT EXIST IN AMERICA?
(Revelation 2:8-11)

<u>Now here was a Congregation of Warriors for Christ.</u>

> *"'I know your tribulation and your poverty (but you are rich) and the slander of those who say that they are Jews and are not, but are a synagogue of Satan. Do not fear what you are about to suffer. Behold, the devil is about to throw some of you into prison, that you may be tested, and for ten days you will have tribulation. Be faithful unto death, and I will give you the crown of life.* **Revelation 2:9-10**

Key Points:

Now here was a congregation of Warriors for Christ

➢ As we contemplate the **tribulation**, the **poverty**, and the **persecution** that this church was experiencing day after day and year after year and **seeing them maintain their faithfulness in Christ**, it should be an awakening to us in the western world.

➢ These Christians who were shortly to be thrown in prison and subsequently killed, Jesus praises them and calls them "rich" and tells them to "fear not" for He endured a similar fate.

➢ Note that He didn't promise to deliver them from their tribulations, but that He would stand with them and strengthen them through it.

Do Smyrna-Committed Churches Exist in America?

➢ <u>Not yet</u> – but, they do currently exist in nations where governments and pagan religions are persecuting the uncompromising Christians.

➢ This is happening daily in Africa, Indonesia, China, India, Pakistan, and also in the Middle Eastern nations.

Notes:
_____
_____
_____
_____
_____

THE CHURCH OF SMYRNA --- DOES IT EXIST IN AMERICA?

Key Points:

The Smyrna churches are compromised of Christians who:

➤ Suffered the loss of their homes and possessions, undergone rejections, blasphemies, and tribulation, and yet have remained steadfastly faithful.

➤ Unlike their Ephesian neighbors, **they have maintained their first love** despite tremendously adverse circumstances.

An Eternal Perspective for these Churches:

➤ These are victorious and conquering churches in the ongoing spiritual war that cannot be hurt by the "second death".

➤ The Smyrna Church teaches us the spiritual character that Jesus Christ values in His people - faithfulness during intense trials.

➤ The tribulation experience not only produces mature and strong Christians, it will also weed out the tares from within their midst.

Where is Jesus when Christians are undergoing tribulation?

➤ He's standing right alongside of us, strengthening and **encouraging us to keep fighting against the powers of darkness** and promising us that the finish line is fast approaching which will **bring eternal rewards so great that our finite minds cannot comprehend them.**[1]

➤ *"Blessed are you when people hate you and when they exclude you and revile you and spurn your name as evil, on account of the Son of Man! **Rejoice in that day**, and leap for joy, for behold**, your reward is great in heaven**; for so their fathers did to the prophets.*
Luke 6:22-23

Notes:

_____

_____

_____

BREAK-TIME   **(Slides # 15 - 16)**

---

[1] Psalm 23:4; 1 Corinthians 2:9; Matthew 5:11-12

(Slides # 17 - 20)

THE CHURCH OF SARDIS --- DOES IT EXIST IN AMERICA?
(Revelation 3:1-6)

Listen to the very first statement that Jesus says to the Sardis church:

……"'*I know your works. You have the reputation of being alive, but you are dead.*
Revelation 3:1

> Something is seriously wrong with this one - yet the Sardis Church had **a reputation in the community for being "alive".**

Key Points:

Envision a Sardis Church in Today's American Culture?

> The church leadership might host a weekly television program

> Her parking lot is full every Sunday and local police are there directing traffic.

> It is a dynamo of activity; programs abound; but it's all done by human effort.

> The Sardis community sends their children to Christian schools, listens to the latest Christian music, attends church on Sundays, **but deep within this people, there is no real hunger for the Lord;**

> Sardis-style churches portray an appearance of spirituality to the world, but God sees into the heart- their works are dead in His sight.

> This church is no different from any worldly club or organization which continually offers great programs to the community.

> Because of these ongoing, non-stop activities, the church gains a reputation for being "alive;" but it is a church that is "dead" in the eyes of the Lord.

Leadership within these Mega-Churches:

> These churches are led by **very gifted "communicators.**

> The Sardis-type churches are led by those who have **lowered the standard of their message to the level of people's sensitivities** in order to make the message nice and inoffensive.

> They believe that being consistent and **strong in the gospel message will not make friends,** fill their **wallets,** or grow **mega-churches.**

Notes:

_____
_____
_____
_____
_____

When Persecution Threatens these Churches:

When this type of church is confronted with **persecution from a worldly government**, the majority will not have the spiritual strength to stand against it and will in fact, **compromise the Gospel message to meet government standards in order to maintain their popularity within the new world system.**

Notes:

_____
_____
_____
_____
_____

Faithful Remnant within this Church:

> ➤ *Yet you have still a few names in Sardis, people who have not soiled their garments, and they will walk with me in white, for they are worthy.* **Revelation 3:4**

> ➤ Like the Ephesian churches, there is a remnant of those within the church who know the love of Christ, but **they are a minority and not the leading element within the church**.

Notes:

_____
_____
_____
_____
_____

(Slides # 21 - 25)

CHURCH OF PHILADELPHIA ---- DOES IT EXIST IN AMERICA?
(Revelation 3:7-13)

Characteristics of the Philadelphia Church:

> *"'I know your works. Behold, I have set before you an open door, which no one is able to shut. <u>I know that you have but little power, and yet you have kept my word and have not denied my name.</u>*
> *Behold, I will make those of the synagogue of Satan who say that they are Jews and are not, but lie— behold, I will make them come and bow down before your feet and they will learn that I have loved you.*
> ***Revelation 3:8-9***

Key Points:

<u>**Like the Smyrna church, this was a church beloved of the Lord.**</u>

➢ A passion for the Lord was the primary focus of their service.

➢ It was a church of "little strength" - a small congregation; with little financial resources.

➢ Yet, it was a church that remained faithful to the truth of the gospel even when they were continually ridiculed by the legalistic Jews

➢ It takes great spiritual strength to continually proclaim the name of the Lord in the midst of ridicule and threats of persecution.

➢ Those who will stand for His truths in such circumstances are the <u>true "overcomers"</u> whom Jesus encourages throughout His letters to the churches.

Notes:
_____
_____
_____
_____
_____
_____

CHURCH OF PHILADELPHIA ---- DOES IT EXIST IN AMERICA?

Kept from the "Hour of Trial"

Jesus told these Philadelphians that because they patiently kept the Word of the Lord, **He would keep them from the "hour of trial" that is coming on the whole world in order to "test" those who dwell upon the earth. (Rev 3:10)**

Key Points:

Perhaps this was a church in a province of Asia Minor that was governed by Roman authorities **that were not persecutors of Christianity**.

➢ Perhaps our Lord restrained persecution for the Philadelphia church in order to allow it to freely proclaim the gospel message throughout the Mediterranean world.

Now these words of Jesus have also been used to support the modern-day theory of a pre-tribulation rapture.

➢ Our first question regarding this should be: why should the church of Smyrna, which was also dearly beloved of the Lord, be cast into the midst of tribulation while the church of Philadelphia is excused?

➢ This "escapism doctrine" of modern day "rapturists" is dangerous.

➢ The church that expects to be received in the air before the great tribulation does not prepare itself for the battle – and in the coming days of temptation, many will fall away; not fly away.

Jesus is not saying that the faithful church will be kept from tribulation but that in the midst of persecution, when the enemy rages - and the temptation to deny the Lord is strong, the Lord will be right alongside to encourage and strengthen His church so that it will endure to the very end.

Christians Warriors will not Compromise Under Threat of Persecution:

➢ **It takes great spiritual strength to continually proclaim the name of the Lord** in the **midst of ridicule and threats of persecution**. Those who will stand for His truths in such circumstances **are the true "overcomers"** that Jesus encourages throughout His letters to the churches.

Notes:

_____

_____

_____

(Slides # 26 - 30)

THE CHURCH OF LAODICEA --- DOES IT EXIST IN AMERICA?
(Revelation 3:14-22)

Jesus begins His message to the Laodicean church with the following statement:

> "'I know your works: you are neither cold nor hot. Would that you were either cold or hot! So, because you are <u>lukewarm</u>, and neither hot nor cold, I will spit you out of my mouth.
> ***Revelation 3:15-16***

Key Points:

Laodiceans have a Lukewarm Love for Jesus:

➢ What was missing in Laodicea is very similar to what is missing in many congregations today - a relationship with Jesus Christ

➢ Laodicean leadership <u>understand foundational theology</u> and <u>express belief</u> in the Lord, but if anyone speaks with them about pursuing a deeper relationship with Jesus, they will quickly label them charismatic fanatics.

➢ A very controlling leadership and those who <u>disagree</u> with their direction for the church <u>are strongly encouraged to leave</u>.

➢ Contrary to what they say, the priorities of these church leaders are not intimacy with Christ but watching Sunday attendance climb, along with the size of the offering.

➢ This leadership is very similar to those in the Ephesian and Sardis-style churches.

➢ More time is spent *organizing* programs than *agonizing* in intercessory prayer. Intercessors have been elbowed aside by intellectuals, who are determined to run the church like a business.

Jesus continues to address this lukewarm attitude when He says:

> *For you say, I am rich, I have prospered, and I need nothing, not realizing that you are wretched, pitiable, poor, blind, and naked.* ***Revelation 3:17***

Notes:

_____
_____
_____

THE CHURCH OF LAODICEA --- DOES IT EXIST IN AMERICA?

The church, not the Lord, has won the hearts of this people; their <u>unspoken attitude may be verbalized as follows</u>:

"Wow, thanks God for the gospel of Jesus Christ. We can take it from here. We appreciate the greatness of Your sacrifice, but now we want to show You what we can do. By the way, if Jesus wants to come with us, He's sure welcome. Again thanks, we'll let you know if we need any additional help."

The God who deeply desires a relationship with His Bride and is jealous for His holiness **has been elbowed aside and replaced by a happier faced model of Christ** who always smiles approvingly at whatever we say or do.

➤ How could anyone who has met the living God, become lukewarm about Him?

Yet, despite their luke-warmness, Christ continues to knock on the door of their hearts.

Those whom I love, I reprove and discipline, so be zealous and repent. Behold, I stand at the door and knock. If anyone hears my voice and opens the door, I will come in to him and eat with him, and he with me. **Revelation 3:19-20**

➤ We need to become not only His subjects but also His children. He is our Lord and King, but He's also our Father.

➤ But, unless the individuals of this church awaken and respond to His knocking, they will remain lukewarm and thus, a terrifying time lies ahead; <u>**He will spit them out of His mouth for this is a church that is nauseating to the Lord.**</u>

<u>**The Laodicean Church is commonplace in America today; they have repackaged God so as to make Him user friendly.**</u>

Notes:
_____
_____
_____
_____
_____

BREAK-TIME   (Slides # 31 - 32)

PRE-TRIBULATION RAPTURE MYTH ---
"THE TRUTH IS LEFT BEHIND"

The pre-tribulation rapture is <u>not an historical teaching</u>, but a modern day teaching that has been adopted by numerous American churches in the 20th century.

➢ In brief, it teaches that Jesus will silently and suddenly return and rapture His church to keep them from a seven-year tribulation during which the rest of humanity must face the Antichrist. At the end of seven years, Jesus will again return visibly to deliver those who became Christians during the tribulation.

Origin of the Pre-Tribulation Rapture Doctrine:

➢ This very deceptive teaching was originally developed in England by John Nelson Darby, who founded the Plymouth Brethren movement back in the mid-1800's and was subsequently made popular in this country by C.I Schofield, a wealthy American attorney who embraced this teaching and felt it should be part of the bible.

➢ Thus, he **published the Schofield Bible** in the early 1900's which contained notes that emphasized this pre-tribulation rapture myth.

➢ Soon thereafter, this misleading doctrine was being taught in various seminaries beginning at Dallas Theological Seminary where Schofield himself was on the board of directors.

➢ Subsequently, this Schofield Bible became very popular among evangelicals, particularly in the charismatic-style churches, many of whom failed to see the difference between a man-made commentary and the inspired word of God since it was all included in a single book.

_____
_____
_____
_____

<u>Pre-tribulation rapture teachings certainly appear to be one of the "myths" that the Lord's Word has warned us about:</u>

*For the time is coming when people will not endure sound teaching, but having itching ears they will accumulate for themselves teachers to suit their own passions, and <u>will turn away from listening to the truth and wander off into **myths**</u>. As for you, always be sober-minded, endure suffering, do the work of an evangelist, fulfill your ministry. 2 Timothy 4:3-5*

So, what is the true result of this mythical teaching – "The Truth is Left Behind"

CONSEQUENCES OF PRE-TRIBULATION RAPTURE TEACHINGS

> **Now, this pre-tribulation rapture theory is more than simple error; it is a deception that can do great damage to one's faith.**
>
> - Many American Christians have been watching the early birth pains convinced by their teachers that the next coming event would be the rapture of the church, yet what is coming in reality is intense persecution for those who hold fast to their faith in Christ.
>
> - A consequence of this mythical teaching will be widespread disillusionment when tribulation descends on this nation and many in the church will believe that they have been deceived by their teachers.
>
> - This can certainly result in a great falling away and many former church-goers will align with the world in blaming God for allowing such catastrophe to take place and will then betray many who remain in the fellowship of the church.

All false prophecies are dangerous, and this one carries particular risks. **Consider the following testimony of Corrie Ten Boom** who was imprisoned by the German Nazi's for hiding Jews from their persecutors; and after the war, spent time as a missionary to the Far East:

> *I have been in countries where the saints are already suffering terrible persecution. In China, the Christians were told: "Don't worry, before the tribulation comes, you will be raptured." Then came a terrible persecution. Millions of Christians were tortured to death. Later I heard a bishop from China say, sadly: "We have failed. We should have made the people strong for persecution rather than telling them Jesus would come first." Turning to me, he said: "Tell the people how to be strong in times of persecution, how to stand when the tribulation comes – to stand and not faint." I feel I have a divine mandate to go and tell the people of this world that it is possible to be strong in the Lord Jesus Christ. We are in training for the tribulation.* [2]

Folks, pre-tribulation rapture teachings are putting the Church at ease when, in fact, **it should be spiritually preparing itself for the greatest battle in the history of mankind.**

Notes:

_____
_____
_____
_____
_____
_____

---

[2] David Pawson, When Jesus Returns (Hodder & Stoughton; 1995) p.199-200

PRE-TRIBULATION RAPTURE – CHRISTIANS "WAKE UP!"

- Historically God's people have experienced intense suffering.

- With the exception of John, all the disciples of Jesus were brutally murdered.

- Thousands of early Christians were mocked, spit on, and torn to shreds by wild animals inside the Coliseum.

- Millions of others were horribly tortured and burned at the stake during the Dark Ages.

- During this age, believers in Russia & China have suffered terribly under communism and so have many faithful followers of Christ in some Muslim countries.

- This is ongoing today in many nations of the world.

Key Points:

We need to 'wake up" - the Christian church is in the midst of spiritual warfare – a war that tests the true faith of God's chosen people.

- In other words, will Christians remain faithful and trust in the Lord during times of tribulation - or will they compromise their faith.

God's greatest commandment is revealed in times of tribulation.

- That is: we are called to love the Lord with all our heart, all our soul, all our mind, and with all of our strength.

- Times of tribulation reveals the priorities of our heart – either love of self or love of God?

Notes:
_____
_____
_____
_____
_____

PRE-TRIBULATION RAPTURE – "A MARINE'S VIEW"

Pre-Trib Rapture Teachings are not for Soldiers in His Army:

- Being a retired Marine Corps officer who spent two tours in the war zones of Vietnam, I disrespect this pre-tribulation rapture myth for being a wimpy sales presentation designed to please those who are scared of potential conflict.

- Marines don't leave people behind on the battlefield and I do get passionately angry when I see Jesus being portrayed as a Commander who calls His people to run from the battle.

- Jesus Christ is the greatest Leader that walked this earth - "**retreat**" is not in His vocabulary.

This Pre-Trib Rapture Beliefs is a Shameful Scenario for God's Mighty Warriors:

- Imagine being a warrior in the Army of God who was raptured before the great battle begins. How would you feel in the presence of those who were martyred for their gospel testimony of Jesus Christ as the Son of God?

- Are those who escape tribulation by being raptured more privileged in God's eyes than those who were martyred for their uncompromising faith?

- Personally, I believe that I would be eternally ashamed to stand alongside my martyred brothers and sisters if I was among one of the privileged saints who were raptured. In fact, we should all be truly grateful for the sacrifice they endured on the battlefield of this life.

- For without these Christian warriors that historically fought for the truths proclaimed by Jesus Christ, Americans would not have the religious freedoms that we have today. Freedoms that have allowed to true gospel message to be proclaimed worldwide over the last 300 years.

Tribulation Results in a Final Great Harvest in the Kingdom of God:

- The tribulation is not something for believers to enjoy; however, it is not something for us to escape from either.

- The primary purpose for times of tribulation is to present an opportunity for lost people to come to repentance; for it is a period of time that will bring in the final harvest. For when God's judgments fall on the world, many will turn to righteousness.[3]

- Thus, God's warriors need to embrace ministry opportunities during a period of tribulation for it is the most important mission we could possibly be assigned.

---

[3] Isaiah 26:9

(Slide # 41)

MIGHTY MEN WITHIN THE DISPENSATIONAL COMMUNITY

Finally, I do want to mention that several fine men of God, who have been raised and schooled in pre-tribualtion rapture doctrines, **are among the very best Christian teachers concerning ongoing current events** in the 21st century.

Men like Hal Lindsey, David Reagan, Chuck Missler, Joel Rosenberg, Greg Laurie, and others have produced tremendously fruitful works. These are "watchmen" in the Army of God. **They have provided significant strategic information for the American church over the last thirty years.**

- Over the last thirty years, believers in the pre-tribulation rapture have been **the most prominent teachers of the Great tribulation events** which lie shortly before us.

- They had the **advantage of teaching hard truths without scaring their listeners** because of the "rapture" beliefs.

- Unfortunately, **much of their message is falling upon "itchy ears" that see no need to prepare.** This is a great danger that I perceive will soon confront the American churches.

We need to embrace the hard message of Matthew 24:9-14 for those days are rapidly approaching American Christianity.

Notes – Consider how you would lovingly speak to others who adhere to pre-tribulation rapture beliefs: (Also note - there are numerous books that expose this false doctrine).

_____
_____
_____
_____
_____
_____
_____

BREAK-TIME   **(Slides # 42 - 43)**

(Slide # 44)

BETRAYAL ARISES FROM WITHIN THE CHURCH

> ➢ *"Then they will deliver you up to tribulation and put you to death, and you will be hated by all nations for my name's sake.*
> ➢ *And **<u>then many will fall away and betray one another</u>** and hate one another. And many false prophets will arise and lead many astray.*
> ➢ *And because lawlessness will be increased, the love of many will grow cold.*
> ➢ *But the one who endures to the end will be saved.*
> ➢ *And this gospel of the kingdom will be proclaimed throughout the whole world as a testimony to all nations, and then the end will come. **Matthew 24:9-14***

This is one of the most eye-opening teachings in the bible when the Lord Jesus informs His disciples that when the nations commence persecuting the church prior to His second coming, many within the church will fall away and hate and betray, those who remain.

➢ This is primarily the **consequence of many false teachers** who are solidly established within the organized church system, but whose teachings continually lead their followers astray.

➢ Yet, the **promise of eternal salvation** is to those who will remain steadfast and not compromise their faith.

Here our Lord Jesus is alerting His people that many of the enemy are within their midst, yet His words are largely ignored within the American church.

➢ However, this is such a huge event that God's kingdom people will face in the near future that it simply cannot be ignored any longer – we need to **"be ready."**

Notes:
_____
_____
_____
_____
_____
_____

(Slide # 45)

THREE PEOPLE GROUPS EMERGE DURING TIMES OF WAR

> Key Points:
>
> Over the last fifty years in America, every war we have fought (particularly Vietnam) has produced three groups of people within this nation.
>
> ➤ **The first group** is comprised of pacifists - those people who will not fight but neither will they protest. (Wimpy types!)
>
> ➤ **The second group** comprises the anti-war demonstrators, who rebel against the call of their country and ridicule those who answer the call. Their motto: "Make love, not war!"
>
> ➤ **The third group** comprises those who willingly, proudly, and bravely step up to answer the call of their country as well as those who strongly support these American warriors who love and believe in their country.

Notes – Consider peoples you know & how you might lovingly speak (not debate) with them concerning their beliefs which causes blindness within themselves.

_____
_____
_____
_____
_____
_____
_____

Now, there is an interesting parallel between these three groups and similar groups found within the American church of today. For example:

(Slides # 46 - 49)

THREE CHURCH GROUPS EMERGE DURING TIMES OF WAR

Key Points:

THE FIRST GROUP

- Comprised of pacifists regularly attends church and Bible studies, but they have little personal vision for ministry.

THE SECOND GROUP

- Actively opposes any talk of warfare. "Make love, not war" is also the motto within their hearts.

- The sinfulness of man and the need for repentance and obedience to Christ is not a powerful voice in these churches. Their self-indulgent and prosperity teachings appeal to many who place their hope in this world.

- Their primary concern is to not offend people and hurt their feelings, and they repeatedly emphasize that Christ has already accomplished the victory for us; so, we just need to be faithful in our tithing and church attendance, and He will provide for all of our needs.

THE THIRD GROUP

- Comprised of warrior-spirited Christians who voluntarily serve in the Army of God.

- These are disciples who are very passionate for Jesus Christ and the Kingdom of God and are prepared to lay down their lives if called upon to do so.

- They are among those who <u>hunger and thirst for righteousness</u>.

- They are among those who <u>mourn</u> over the abominations that are committed in this country and also in many of our churches.

- Yet, they are among those who <u>love their enemies</u> and pray for those who persecute them

- These are the ones who will fight the war against the forces of darkness that rules over the kingdom of this world and keeps many of our family, friends, and co-workers in bondage.

Their heart's desire is to be among their fellow soldiers who embrace the following words of our Lord:
Matthew 5:11-16
- <u>Blessed are you when others revile you and persecute you</u> and utter all kinds of evil against you falsely on my account.
- <u>Rejoice and be glad</u>, for your reward is great in heaven, for so they persecuted the prophets who were before you.

> You are the light of the world. A city set on a hill cannot be hidden. Nor do people light a lamp and put it under a basket, but on a stand, and it gives light to all in the house.
> In the same way, let your light shine before others, so that they may see your good works and give glory to your Father who is in heaven.

Now, how will each of these three groups respond when suddenly, like a thief in the night, catastrophic events occur that destroy this nation's economy and cause the loss of a great number of lives, and robs us of the freedom that we once enjoyed?

Notes:

_____
_____
_____
_____
_____
_____
_____
_____
_____
_____
_____
_____
_____
_____

With this background, consider who are those that Jesus warned us about when He said

"In the Last Days Many Will Fall Away and Betray Others"

Consider the parable of the sower who went out to sow seed – seed being the Word of God:

(Slide # 50)

THE FIRST GROUP – "SEED SOWN ON ROCKY GROUND"

Key Points:

The first group of pacifists is like the "seed sown on rocky ground."

➤ They can be found in many of the Laodicean-style churches – "Those with a lukewarm faith."

Listen to Jesus teach His disciples concerning this group:

As for what was sown on rocky ground, this is the one who hears the word and immediately receives it with joy, yet he has no root in himself, but endures for a while, and when tribulation or persecution arises on account of the word, immediately he falls away. **Matthew 13:20-21**

➤ How will this group respond when faced with tribulation --- will they "fall away" and "betray others" within the church?

(Slide # 51)

THE SECOND GROUP – "SEED SOWN AMONG THORNS"

Key Points:

The second group of liberal, anti-war activists is like the "seed sown among thorns."

➤ They love to attend many of the Sardis-style churches – "Those who believe they are rich, but are poor."

Listen to Jesus teach His disciples concerning this group:

And as for what fell among the thorns, they are those who hear, but as they go on their way they are choked by the cares and riches and pleasures of life, and their fruit does not mature. **Luke 8:14**

➤ How will this group respond when faced with tribulation --- will they "fall away" and "betray others" within the church?

(Slide # 52)

THE THIRD GROUP – "SEED SOWN IN FERTILE SOIL"

The third group of uncompromising Christians who stand strong for the Kingdom of God is like "seed sown in fertile soil."

> They can be found in many of the Smyrna and Philadelphia-style churches -"Those who overcome the world."

Listen to Jesus teach His disciples concerning this group:
As for what was sown on good soil, this is the one who hears the word and understands it. He indeed bears fruit and yields, in one case a hundredfold, in another sixty, and in another thirty." **Matthew 13:23**

Notes – Consider these people groups in your respective environments & how to minister to those in each of these three groups:

(Slides # 53 - 54)

"CHRISTIANS" – A TIME OF DECISION IS COMING SOON

Jesus is a great army Commander who is giving instructions to His soldiers; however, some of the officers under His command are giving contrary instructions preparing for a massive retreat.

➢ A soldier preparing for war is very different than the one who thinks he will be discharged shortly before the war begins. Many believers today are like soldiers looking forward to an early discharge.

➢ Can you imagine David or Joshua preparing their soldiers to retreat when the heat turns up? Can you imagine Peter or Paul looking to escape from preaching the gospel because persecution was coming?

During a Period of Intense Tribulation –

<u>Will we be among those who:</u>
……. will fall away and betray one another and hate one another. And many false prophets will arise and lead many astray. And because lawlessness will be increased, the love of many will grow cold. **Matthew 24:10-12**

<u>Or, will our hearts respond with:</u>
My soul yearns for you in the night; my spirit within me earnestly seeks you. For when your judgments are in the earth, the inhabitants of the world learn righteousness. **Isaiah 26:9**

<u>And</u>:
"Blessed are you when others revile you and persecute you and utter all kinds of evil against you falsely on my account. Rejoice and be glad, for your reward is great in heaven, for so they persecuted the prophets who were before you. **Matthew 5:11-12**

Notes:
_____
_____
_____
_____
_____

"ABOUT FACE"

Those with military experience are very familiar with the command "about-face" which is a command to immediately turn sharply 180 degrees from the direction you are currently facing.

- ➤ It is also a command used by our Commander-in-Chief **who calls us to "turn" from our sins**; then He will remove the veil which is blinding us from the truth and put us on the path of growing in spiritual maturity.

- ➤ This willingness to turn in an **"about-face" will suddenly cause us to see ourselves as we truly are and thus, our need for a Savior.**

- ➤ **All of God's champions will occasionally go astray** and veer from the course that the Lord directs. However, like Moses, David, or Paul, **they all have one thing in common**; when confronted with their blindness, they will readily turn in an "about-face" and return to following their Commander.

What will Christians do when our Commander-in-Chief commands us to "about-face"?

- ➤ Will they obey Him or listen to other subordinate commanders, such as some church leaders who tell us that the Commander-in-Chief really meant **"right-face"** since it is much easier to follow that path.

- ➤ **But a partial turn will eventually lead us away from the path that Jesus is going** and even though other leaders tell us that we are moving rightly, we are straying further and further from His direction.

- ➤ Some other false commanders may convince us that the command was really **"at-ease"**; just keep coming and giving to the church and God will be pleased.

- ➤ Eventually the time comes when the Commander-in-Chief gives the command **"forward march"**; only those who heard and obeyed the command **"about-face"** will be equipped to follow the King of kings and the Lord of lords in the direction He is heading.[4]

---

[4] Al Houghton, *Word at Work* (Newsletter Volume XXI, Number IX, Chapter 10)

(Slide # 56)

THE NEXT SESSION:

SEALS / HORSEMEN / MARTYRDOM

First Read: Revelation 4 – 5 - 6

- ➢ The opening of the first "Five Seals" and their Effect on the World of Today.

- ➢ Identifying the Four Horsemen and their Respective Missions

- ➢ The Positive & Negative Effect of the Four Horsemen

- ➢ Looking at a World without the Four Horsemen

- ➢ A Christian perspective on Tribulation

- ➢ We'll also meet the "Martyrs under the Throne" as the Fifth Seal is Opened and their lesson for Christian warriors of this generation.

- ➢ The Spirit of Martyrdom

- ➢ Today's Scoffers will be Tomorrow's Persecutors

- ➢ The Lamb of God is our True Commander-in-Chief

THE LAMB OF GOD - OUR TRUE "COMMANDER-IN-CHIEF"

The days are rapidly approaching when a tremendous separation will take place among mankind.

Yet, during this present era of warfare, He reigns as our Commander-in-Chief and His Name continues to be the battle cry for those warriors who fight daily for righteousness and truth.

His name is Jesus, Our Lord, Our King, Our Commander-in-Chief

- A truly mighty Leader who would never delegate assignments to His people that He Himself wouldn't readily embrace.

- A Commander that Christian warriors will readily follow not matter the danger or what costs have to be paid.

- These are warriors whose deepest desire is to hear Jesus welcome them with the following words when they enter into His presence:

> .... 'Well done, good and faithful servant. You have been faithful over a little; I will set you over much. Enter into the joy of your master.' *Matthew 25:21*

SEALS / HORSEMEN / And MARTYRDOM

(Revelation 4 – 5 – 6)

SESSION #3 – WORKBOOK
Intended For
"KINGDOM WARRIORS IN THE ARMY OF GOD"

Unveiling Mysteries in the "Book of Revelation"

Based upon the Book:
GOD'S ANOINTED WARRIORS
By
Dr. Donald Bell
Major USMC, Ret.

(Slides # 2 - 5)

BOOK OF REVELATION = INTELLIGENCE FOR HIS ARMY

Enlistment in the Army of God requires a foundational understanding of the battles that are coming and our missional assignments.

Key Points:

Jesus Christ has provided His soldiers with detailed intelligence concerning events preceding His return to reign over the nations of the earth.

➤ This intelligence has primarily been recorded in the book of Revelation, which promises great blessings to those who will believe and keep the words of this prophetic book.

➤ For Christians to voluntarily enlist in this endeavor, they need to have a foundational understanding of the battles that are coming and the mission to which they are called.

➤ The large majority of mankind in both the church and the nations will soon be overwhelmed by sudden catastrophic events that will forever change their habitual lifestyles - from a life rooted in relative ease and comfort, to one of extreme hardships with many challenges that must be confronted in order to survive.

➤ Christian soldiers need to be equipped and ready to be deployed into their respective missional assignments that await them.

➤ However, in order for Christians to voluntarily enlist in this endeavor, they need to have a foundational understanding of the battles that are coming and their respective missions to which they are called

---

The following words spoken to Daniel concerning the "last days" are meant to encourage this army of warriors.

Those who are wise shall shine like the brightness of the sky above; and those who turn many to righteousness, like the stars forever and ever. **(Daniel 12:3)**

Notes:
_____
_____
_____
_____
_____

(Slides # 6 - 7)

TRIUNE SERIES OF CHAOTIC EVENTS

<u>Key Points:</u>

In The Book Of Revelation, There Is A Triune Series Of Catastrophic Events That Are Released By The Power Of Our Lord As:

- The breaking of the "seven seals of the scroll which affects 1/4 of the earth."
- The blowing of the "seven trumpets which affects 1/3 of the earth!"
- The pouring out of the "seven bowls of wrath which affects the entire earth!"

Additionally, there appears to be acceleration as the events unfold:

- The seven seals seem quite spread out in time.
- The subsequent series of trumpets and bowls appear to be measured in months or even days.
- Also, the three series are successive; that is, they follow on the heels of one another.

Finally, there are very important interludes within this succession of events:

- The threefold series of seals, trumpets, and bowls are primarily concerned with what will happen to the world.
- These interludes give us insight into how God's people are affected during this threefold series of events and our calling in the midst of it.

Notes:

(Slides # 8 - 9)

THE SEVEN SEALS – AN OVERVIEW

When our Lord Jesus takes the scroll from the hands of His Father and proceeds to break the seals of the scroll, it appears to have three effects:

1. The opening of the seals <u>reveals the effect that the gospel message</u> of the Lord Jesus Christ will have on different segments of peoples in the world throughout the centuries.

2. Secondly, it provides us with insight into <u>God's purposes for releasing those events</u> that will usher in the Kingdom of God throughout the earth.

3. Third, <u>it appears to physically launch these events.</u>

Key Points:

Now the opening of the scroll is intended to reveal to our generation the main aspects of our future, as well as the history of the Christian era, as these forces cooperate to bring the kingdom of Christ to its perfect consummation.

➢ The breaking of the **"first five seals" began in the first century** at the time the Gospel of Christ first went out into the world, or very shortly thereafter.

➢ Their great power continues to affect the world to this day. Jesus refers to these afflictions as "merely the beginning of birth pangs;" yet, they appear to continue right up to the period of the Great Tribulation.[5] A period that culminates with the coming of Jesus Christ to establish His kingdom upon this earth.

➢ **The "sixth and seventh seals" have not yet been broken,** but their time is rapidly approaching.

Notes:

_____
_____
_____
_____
_____

---

[5] Matthew 24:8-9

(Slides # 10 - 11)

THE OLIVET DISCOURSE & SIX SEALS OF THE SCROLL

The teaching of Jesus on the Mt of Olives in Matthew 24 and Luke 21 outlines the chaotic events which precede His 2nd coming to establish the Kingdom of God on this earth. This teaching is widely referred to as the "Olivet Discourse."

For example:

- False messengers of the gospel would arise and deceive many who are seeking truths

- There would be an increase in worldwide wars and rumors of wars

- Earthquakes, famines, diseases, and lawlessness would be rampant in the world.

- Uncompromising Christians would be hated by the nations

- The Christian church would experience tribulation and many would be killed.

- This results in a great falling away from the church of those who will betray and hate their former family and friends who remain steadfast in their faith.

- There will be terrors and greats signs in the heavens

- But, Jesus tells us to not be terrified by these multiple tribulations for they must take place before the time of the end.

Notes:
_____
_____
_____
_____
_____
_____
_____
_____

BREAK-TIME   **(Slides # 12 - 13)**

(Slide # 14)

THE FOUR HORSEMEN – AN OVERVIEW

As the first four seals are broken, four horsemen emerge with individual missions which will bring forth much chaos and confusion into the world.

Key Points:

Now, there is difference among commentators as to the identity of the first horseman riding the white horse.

➢ Some believe this represents the gospel of Jesus Christ going forth into the world, and they have generally sound arguments supporting this belief.
➢ Others believe that the white horseman is going forth with the message of the false gospel that Jesus warned us would take place throughout the times leading up to His return.
➢ Both of these views have elements of truth.

Late in the first century when John witnessed the release of these four horsemen, the New Testament epistles had already been written and the true gospel message had been proclaimed throughout the Roman Empire.

➢ Subsequently, false gospel messages became more and more prevalent within the newly formed Christian churches.

Now the next three horsemen riding the red, black, and pale horses are spiritual forces that are mostly obsessed with usurping God's kingdom plans for the earth; yet they are limited by the Lord in their desire to kill and destroy.

Now there is a parallelism between the opening of these seals and the teachings of Jesus on the Mt. of Olives when His disciples were inquiring as to when the Lord would return.

For both portray a spiritual battle that will be fought until the return of our Lord Jesus who will also appear riding on a white horse.

Notes:

_____
_____
_____
_____
_____

(Slides # 15 - 16)

THE FIRST SEAL RELEASES THE RIDER ON THE "WHITE HORSE"

Revelation 6:1-2
Now I watched when the Lamb opened one of the seven seals, and I heard one of the four living creatures say with a voice like thunder, "Come!" And I looked, and behold, a white horse! And its rider had a bow, and a crown was given to him, and he came out conquering, and to conquer.

Key Points:
- This rider on a white horse is a spiritual portrayal of an armed warrior who is being sent onto the battlefield of the world.

- Thus, this horseman on the white horse appears to be symbolic of mighty soldiers in the Army of God who are armed with a bow which will launch numerous arrows carrying the gospel message of Jesus Christ into the hearts of mankind throughout the earth.

- They are conquering warriors that have overcome the world and have a true heart of love for those who are captives of the darkness.

- <u>Victory is assured as indicated by the crown</u> given to this horseman, yet this conquering Army of God must battle through many generations until that day when the Lord Jesus Christ will also appear riding on a white horse

(Slides # 17 - 18)

White Horse Mission –

- To communicate the following message into the hearts of those who will hear :

"For God so loved the world, that he gave his only Son, that whoever believes in him should not perish but have eternal life. **John 3:16**

Deception Follows on the Heals of the White Horsemen

The apostle Paul also warns Christians concerning many false teachers who will arise in the midst of the world in order to deceive those who have heard the message of the white horseman.

For such men are false apostles, deceitful workmen, disguising themselves as apostles of Christ. And no wonder, for even <u>Satan disguises himself as an angel of light</u>. So it is no surprise if his servants, also, disguise themselves as servants of righteousness. Their end will correspond to their deeds. 2 Corinthians 11:13-15

- These are those who will accept many of the doctrines of the bible, but deny that Jesus Christ is the only way to eternal life. **It appears the "false gospel messengers" will also be following on the heels of the "white horse."**

(Slide # 19)

THE SECOND SEAL RELEASES THE RIDER ON THE "RED HORSE"

Revelation 6:3-4
When he opened the second seal, I heard the second living creature say, "Come!" And out came another horse, bright red. Its rider was permitted to take peace from the earth, so that men should slay one another, and he was given a great sword.

Key Points:

Red Horse Mission - To cause continuing worldwide warfare between nations and kingdoms throughout the Christian era.

➢ This has taken place in many forms throughout the last 2,000 years, but has emerged into worldwide wars beginning in the 20th century.

(Slides # 20 - 21)

THE THIRD SEAL RELEASES THE RIDER ON THE "BLACK HORSE"

Revelation 6:5-6
When he opened the third seal, I heard the third living creature say, "Come!" And I looked, and behold, a black horse! And its rider had a pair of scales in his hand. And I heard what seemed to be a voice in the midst of the four living creatures, saying, "A quart of wheat for a denarius, and three quarts of barley for a denarius, and do not harm the oil and wine!"

Key Points:

➢ The scales used for weighing the wheat and the barley are symbolic of limiting food products for the poor populace in various parts of the earth.
➢ The oil and wine appears to represent the food products for the wealthy.

Black Horse Mission - To cause continuing social unrest within nations by utilizing earthly products to maintain enmity between the rich and the poor.

➢ This "black horse" brings drought, famine, and economic hardships to many in the world.
➢ Oil and wine remains untouched which reveals that the wealthy will remain distinct from the masses.

Yet the wealthy continually ignore the cries of the poor in their ongoing addiction for more power and riches.

(Slides # 22 - 23)

THE FOURTH SEAL RELEASES THE RIDER ON THE "PALE HORSE"

Revelation 6:7-8
When he opened the fourth seal, I heard the voice of the fourth living creature say, "Come!" And I looked, and behold, a pale horse! And its rider's name was Death, and Hades followed him. And they were given authority over a fourth of the earth, to kill with sword and with famine and with pestilence and by wild beasts of the earth.

Pale Horse Mission - To follow after the first three horsemen and bring about all forms of unnatural death that will continually affect one-fourth of the world's population.

Key Points:

- The **Red Horseman** is responsible for worldwide wars which have caused millions of casualties over the centuries.

- The poor struggling in hunger, slavery, and various diseases caused by the **Black Horseman** has also resulted in many loss of lives.

- All of these scenarios provide human bodies for the **Pale Horse Rider** who joyfully gathers them up.

- Additionally, churches ruled by false gospel messengers have martyred many of God's uncompromising Christians over the centuries.

- Although they were killed for their uncompromising faith in Christ, Hades has no authority over these Christians as indicated by the 5th seal event.

Notes:

_____
_____
_____
_____
_____
_____
_____
_____

BREAK-TIME **(Slides # 24 - 25)**

(Slide # 26)

THE COMBINED EFFECT OF THE FOUR HORSEMEN UPON THE WORLD
(Revelation 6:1-8)

The four horsemen were released with the opening of the first four seals:

➢ They have been making their drive throughout the earth from the beginning of the Christian era until the present day.

➢ They have repeatedly kept the world in turmoil and will continue to do so with even greater intensity until the Kingdom of God comes in fullness.

Key Points:

Christianity would like to believe that the Lord would not allow His people to be affected by the wars, famines, diseases, and deaths which are caused by the release of the powers commonly referred to as the "four horsemen of the apocalypse." Obviously, this is not the case for all these forces are sent into the world in general and they affect all of mankind.[6]

➢ When the **"red horse"** appears and brings bloodshed and wars, we, as well as the unbelieving world, see our sons go into battle, where many have and will suffer and die.

➢ The same is true of the **"black horse,"** which brings drought, famine, and economic hardships. Whatever steps mankind takes, this economic law cannot be eliminated: as soon as wages increase, the prices of commodities also rise, and the economic division among the people remains the same; rich and poor continue.

➢ This causes divisions in society in the form of strikes, protests, uprisings, and so on.

➢ The **"pale horse"** also enters the homes of the righteous and wicked alike and brings death in all its various forms.

However, the spirits symbolized by these horsemen do appear to affect the non-Christian nations of the world more adversely than those nations that profess a belief in Christianity.

Now God's people handle devastations much different than how people of the world handle it.

So let's examine the Positive & Negative Effects of the Four Horsemen

---

[6] Matthew 13:24-30 (The Parable of the Weeds) - Read

(Slide # 27)

THE EFFECT OF THE TRUE GOSPEL MESSAGE PROCLAIMED BY THE RIDER ON THE WHITE HORSE

The proclamation of the true gospel message of Jesus Christ will have a different effect upon different people:

Key Points:

Upon those who believe this truth and open their hearts to receive the Lord into their lives;

- It will mean a transformation from the powers of darkness into the kingdom of light.

- Thus, Christ's Kingdom grows and is strengthened.

However, this same gospel of truth will also harden the hearts of those who put their faith and trust in the world

- Many will run to the message proclaimed by the false prophets who follow after the rider on the white horse in order to distort the truths.

- The doctrines of this false gospel are found in Roman Catholicism as well as in many liberal protestant denominations.

- Additionally, New Age doctrines are surfacing in many of today's mega-churches which combine the doctrines of worldwide pagan religions with those of Christianity

The Islamic faith also arose out of the proclamation of the gospel.

- However, this message proclaims that their Allah is the same as the God of Abraham.

- This "Chrislam view" is also supported by many false teachers in the "compromised Christian churches" including the pope of Roman Catholicism.

Notes:

_____
_____
_____
_____

(Slide # 28)

THE FALSE GOSPEL – ITS POSITIVE EFFECTS

The positive effect of these false gospel messages visibly reveals a separation between those who truly love God and those who love the man-made religions within the world of Christianity. **That is:**

- Are they seeking God out of a true heart of love with the primary purpose of glorifying Him or seeking Him for worldly riches in this life?

- Does the worship of God take precedence over worshiping their respective churches and denominations?

- Do they desire to follow God as sons and daughters in order to please Him in this life or desire to follow false teachers who tickle their ears and speak guarantees of salvation which allows them to continue in their comfort-seeking, lustful lifestyle?

Key Points:

This division between true and false Christianity visibly reveals the differences between:

- Those who are truly sons and daughters of our heavenly Father and those who are "weeds" which the enemy has sown in the midst of the church.

Without this visible division:

- Religious leadership would evolve, much like the Pharisaic church during the time of Jesus, which would attempt to control the world of Christianity with man-made doctrines that must be followed under the threat of persecution.

- Historically, this has been the mission of the Islamic Faith as well as Roman Catholicism,

But due to this visible separation between the true and false gospel messages,

- True Christianity has not been deceived and continues to stand firm for the Kingdom of God even in the face of extradition and persecution.

Notes:
_____
_____
_____
_____

(Slides # 29 - 30)

RED, BLACK & PALE HORSES
BOTH POSITIVE & NEGATIVE EFFECTS

Key Points:

What is evil to the world may not be evil to the children of God; for example:

➢ The same adversities caused by wars, famine, death, etc. causes some to rise in rebellion and curse God, while others will humble themselves and patiently seek God.

➢ The same affliction can harden some while it brings others to repentance and sanctifies them.

➢ The same tribulation that brings despair to this one causes the other to glorify God.

In summary then, what is the effect of the four horsemen upon mankind?

➢ It tends to cause a visible separation between the people of darkness and the people of light.

➢ The true church grows stronger and purer during times of intense trials and conversely, the ungodly grow deeper and stronger in their hatred toward God and His people.

➢ This has been a proven effect around the globe throughout the last 2,000 years of the Christian era and these trials will become even more intense as the world moves toward the second coming of our Lord.

Notes:

(Slides # 31 - 32)

A WORLD WITHOUT THE FOUR HORSEMEN

What would be the result if there were no wars, no social struggles, and no death in all these forms?
Answer:

➢ The kingdom of darkness would reach the height of its development prematurely.

Key Points:

All things would be under the control of this world-power:

➢ It would force the powers of church and state, of home and school, of business and commerce, to comply with the antichristian order of things.

➢ This world power would leave no standing room for the true church of God on earth. It would persecute and, if possible, destroy the kingdom of God in the world.

Atheism among the world's leaders would like to outlaw all religion, but it cannot since so many peoples that are involved in the false churches and cults would not allow it.

➢ Thus, the false gospel that follows the white horseman is welcomed by the world government since it can be used to assist in wiping out the name of Jesus Christ and the purpose of His crucifixion.

But, as long as nation rises against nation,

➢ World power cannot realize itself, for the simple reason that it labors continually for its own survival amidst ongoing confusion and cannot organize itself in a one world unity.

➢ However, the time will come, and probably quite soon, when the Lord allows a partial realization of this antichristian world power to maintain itself for a brief time, and it is <u>at that time when true Christianity will be social outcasts who are hated throughout the world.</u>

Notes:

_____
_____
_____
_____
_____
_____

(Slides # 33 - 34)

A CHRISTIAN PERSPECTIVE ON TRIBULATION

Obviously, citizens of the kingdom of God also suffer according to the flesh for we too are grieved when our sons die on the battlefield, when our homes and jobs are taken from us, or when our loved ones fall into sinful lifestyle.

As we continue along our journey through the wilderness of life, we discover that our Lord sees persecution from a different perspective than we do.

> *"Blessed are those who are persecuted for righteousness' sake, for theirs is the kingdom of heaven." Blessed are you when others revile you and persecute you and utter all kinds of evil against you falsely on my account. Rejoice and be glad, for your reward is great in heaven, for so they persecuted the prophets who were before you.* **Matthew 5:10-12**

Key Points:

He instructs us over and over about expecting and handling persecution for He knows that affliction brings great strength and maturity to His chosen people.[7]

- He calls us to <u>not only endure persecution</u> from the world, but <u>to actually accept it with great joy</u>; for the glory that awaits is so great that present times of suffering and persecution are not even worthy of our concern.[8]

Historically, during these times of tribulation, the church has grown greater and stronger; for it is a time when the Body of Christ turns fully to the Lord in intercessory prayer.

- Today's churches in China, Africa, the Middle East, Indonesia, and other parts of the world which continually face life-threatening persecution <u>reveals tremendous growth and strength among their people.</u>

- <u>Such churches are obviously much stronger in their love and devotion to the Lord than those in our nation.</u>

Christians realize that all things work together for good for those who love God.[9]

In the midst of devastating and grievous circumstances and even when confronted with death, <u>we are spiritually never harmed</u>; for by faith we cling to <u>our Lord who has a much greater vision for each of us.</u>

---

[7] 2 Timothy 3:12; Romans 5:3-4
[8] James 1:2-4; Romans 8:16-18
[9] Romans 8:28; 1 Corinthians 2:9

(Slides # 35 - 36)

A CHRISTIAN PERSPECTIVE ON TRIBULATION

Key Points:

As we experience the trials of life, the eyes of our faith need to be focused more and more on the glory that awaits us.

- In the midst of grievous circumstances, we are spiritually never harmed; for by faith we cling to our Lord who has a much greater vision for each of us.

- Now it is war, sin, suffering, but presently it will be righteousness, holiness, peace and joy, when the kingdom of Christ comes.

So in times of war and trouble, famine and pestilence, when the "Red Horse" drives through the earth and the "Black Horse" appears in your streets, or the "Pale Horse" enters into your homes,

- Let your hearts rest in the power of our Lord Jesus Christ, Who holds the scroll with the seven seals and controls all things in heaven and on earth.

Remember Paul's words:

For I consider that the sufferings of this present time are not worth comparing with the glory that is to be revealed to us. **Romans 8:18**

Notes:

BREAK-TIME (Slides # 37 - 38)

(Slides # 39 - 42)

THE FIFTH SEAL – SOULS OF THE MARTYRS

When he opened the fifth seal, I saw under the altar the souls of those who had been slain for the word of God and for the witness they had borne. They cried out with a loud voice, "O Sovereign Lord, holy and true, how long before you will judge and avenge our blood on those who dwell on the earth?" Then they were each given a white robe and told to rest a little longer, until the number of their fellow servants and their brothers should be complete, who were to be killed as they themselves had been. **Revelation 6:9-11**

A chief purpose of this seal is to clearly show that the martyrdom of saints is under the control of Jesus Christ and for a necessary element in the ongoing war with the enemies of the Kingdom of God.

➢ These are committed warriors in the army of God that did not hide their light under a basket. They not only testified to the Word of God but they clung to it right up to the point of death.

<u>**A very long list of names certainly exists in heaven for those who were slain for the name and the truth of God in Christ Jesus our Lord. Consider the following:**</u>

➢ The disciples who followed Jesus during His ministry upon this earth, with the exception of John, were all brutally martyred.

➢ The terrible persecutions under the Roman emperors; how those who confessed the name of Christ Jesus were literally butchered and tortured to death.

➢ The forerunners of the Reformation who refused to return to the harlot church of Catholicism; multitudes were burned at the stake by that harlot church which was responsible for the dark ages of the middle centuries.

➢ And today - the countless Christians that are continually murdered in those countries that embrace false religions and live under unrighteous governments.

➢ How they were brought to the scaffold and burned at the stake. How they were stoned. How they were cutup with saws. How they were crucified. How they were skinned alive. How some had their legs and arms pulled from their bodies by horses. How they were clawed and eaten by wild beasts in from of cheering crowds.

➢ This tremendous brutality of worldly governments and religions toward those who will not compromise their faith visibly reflects their evilness and deep hatred for the Lord Almighty and His Son, Jesus Christ.

As you go through history from its very dawn to the present time, you will find an innumerable host under the altar, slain for their love for God and His Son. <u>How precious they are in the presence of the Lord.</u>

(Slides # 43 - 45)

THE SPIRIT OF MARTYRDOM

<u>The biblical word for "a martyr" in the Greek language is "a witness." A 'true spirit' of martyrdom is the willingness to risk all for the benefit of others.</u>

➢ The 'true spirit' of martyrdom is not about dying, it is about faithfulness; that is, it is about dying to self in order to accomplish the risky work of living for Jesus.

What about the Muslim martyrs who are sent on suicidal missions in order to kill their supposed enemies; in the name of their Allah? <u>Well, look at their motive</u>:

➢ It is intentional martyrdom for their own self-glory where they envision eternal carnal delight.
➢ Yes, it is a witness unto death, but <u>it is the "false spirit" of martyrdom</u>.

<u>Muslim martyrs die trying to "kill you"</u>
<u>Christian martyrs die trying to "save you"</u>

➢ The true martyrs are those who lay down their lives for the cause of Christ; they are not the casualties of war; they are the victors.

What is meant by "laying down one's life" for the cause of Christ? Listen carefully:

➢ Christians who are threatened with being executed will be given an opportunity to be set free by their captors if they will just deny the Lord Jesus as the Son of God and the only way to eternal life.

True martyrdom is a powerful witness to the world and through their sacrifice; many people have historically embraced the Lord and entered into the Kingdom of God.

➢ Christians in our generation will likely be confronted with this decision but remember this, the reward that awaits their uncompromising witness will be great.

"Blessed are those who are persecuted for righteousness' sake, for theirs is the kingdom of heaven." Blessed are you when others revile you and persecute you and utter all kinds of evil against you falsely on my account. Rejoice and be glad, for your reward is great in heaven, for so they persecuted the prophets who were before you. **Matthew 5:10-12**

(Slides # 46 - 47)

"HOW LONG, O SOVEREIGN LORD?"

Day and night throughout the centuries, God's intercessors have cried out to the Lord that His kingdom will come and righteous judgment will occur on the earth. **Yet our Lord tarries**.

<u>Key Points:</u>

Though He is at work every moment of every day, it is not always as we wish or in ways that are visible to us.

➢ He is on the <u>throne of justice</u>; so we may wonder just how long justice can be postponed.

➢ Yet we must remember that He is also on the <u>throne of grace</u>. This grace is intended not only for those being persecuted but also for their persecutors.

➢ If postponement of justice for one more day results in bringing one more person into the Kingdom of Christ, then so be it.

➢ If a million years from now we were to ask ourselves whether our momentary suffering during our earthly life was an acceptable exchange for one more soul to enter into eternal glory, how would we answer?

How long must these martyrs wait for the judgment of God to fall on the world?

➢ Until all of their brethren who are yet to be killed, even as they were, is complete.

➢ It simply means the time is not yet ripe for God's judgment because there are still future witnesses (martyrs) for Christ that must allow the testimony of the gospel to go forth.

Ask: are you ready for His return right now?

➢ Unsaved family & friends?

Notes:

_____
_____
_____
_____
_____
_____

(Slides # 48 - 49)

TODAY'S SCOFFERS WILL BE TOMORROW'S PERSECUTORS

The time of the end will witness scoffers who deride any message concerning the return of Christ.

> *...knowing this first of all, that scoffers will come in the last days with scoffing, following their own sinful desires. They will say, "Where is the promise of his coming?* **2 Peter 3:3-4**

Key Points:

We will see this as leftist politicians, major news media, many popular movie stars, plus numerous compromising churches embrace worldly socialistic values and <u>denounce the true Christian church as being a separatist, hate filled, and uncompromising segment of society</u>.

- When the churches in America are confronted with the choice of standing for Jesus Christ or suffering persecution from the government, many will fall away and betray their former friends who will not compromise their love for the Lord.

- <u>Today's scoffers will soon become tomorrow's persecutors</u> of the true believers and followers of Jesus Christ.

The "gray area" of Christianity will soon disappear in America and today's churches will soon be divided as the events contained in the above passages accelerate.

- These are hard truths and the majority of Christians would rather ignore them with the hope it won't happen in their lifetime rather than face the truth and prepare for it as the Lord commanded.

- This is the situation in the churches that Christ's warrior leadership must boldly confront.

> <u>*"Then they will deliver you up to tribulation and put you to death, and you will be hated by all nations for my name's sake.*</u> *And then many will fall away and betray one another and hate one another. And many false prophets will arise and lead many astray. And because lawlessness will be increased, the love of many will grow cold. But the one who endures to the end will be saved. And this gospel of the kingdom will be proclaimed throughout the whole world as a testimony to all nations, and then the end will come.* **Matthew 24:9-14**

(Slide # 50)

WHEN WILL THE LORD'S JUDGMENT COME?

Key Points:

The world has not yet shown its real character in the fullness of its hatred of God, the Father and His Son.

➤ However, the time is coming when the world populace will be fully conscious that it is the hateful name of Jesus Christ that is the great obstacle for all their plans of globalization.

➤ The world must attack the true body of Christ in full conscientiousness that it is making an attack on the holiness and the truth of God.

➤ There will be no more gray area between good and evil; one either stands with Him or against Him.

➤ Separation of the two kingdoms will become completely visible to all. It is at this point that the world is ripe for judgment.

Yet, it will not occur in the United States until the following takes place:

➤ When the government of this country which was founded upon Christian values joins with the rest of the world in its hatred toward true Christianity and the nation of Israel.

➤ Those with discernment understand that contemporary America is currently on the precipice of uniting against the Lord's people.

Notes:

(Slide # 51)

THE LAMB OF GOD IS OUR TRUE COMMANDER-IN-CHIEF

> **His name is Jesus, our Lord and our King. He is our Commander-in-Chief.**
>
> ➢ A truly mighty Leader who would never delegate assignments to His people that He Himself wouldn't readily embrace.
>
> ➢ A Commander who true Christian warriors will readily follow no matter the danger, or what battles have to be confronted, or what costs have to be paid.
>
> ➢ These are warriors whose deepest desire in this life is to love Him with all of our hearts, all of our souls, all of our minds, and with all of our strength.
>
> ➢ And to hear Jesus welcome them with the following words when they enter into His presence:

*'Well done, good and faithful servant. You have been faithful over a little; I will set you over much. Enter into the joy of your master.' **Matthew 25:21***

(Slide # 52)

THE NEXT SESSION:

THE 6TH SEAL – A GREAT WAR IS COMING

First Read: Revelation 6:12-17 & Ezekiel 38 & 39

> ➢ The Opening of the 6th Seal
> ➢ The Entire World will Acknowledge the Reality of God
> ➢ A Great War Begins in the Middle East
> ➢ God's Purpose for Israel
> ➢ A Mighty Army Descends upon Israel
> ➢ The Invasion from the North & the Lord's Response
> ➢ Catastrophic Events will Follow this War
> ➢ World War & The Christian Attitude

THE LAMB OF GOD - OUR TRUE "COMMANDER-IN-CHIEF"

The days are rapidly approaching when a tremendous separation will take place among mankind.

Yet, during this present era of warfare, He reigns as our Commander-in-Chief and His Name continues to be the battle cry for those warriors who fight daily for righteousness and truth.

His name is Jesus, Our Lord, Our King, Our Commander-in-Chief

- A truly mighty Leader who would never delegate assignments to His people that He Himself wouldn't readily embrace.

- A Commander that Christian warriors will readily follow not matter the danger or what costs have to be paid.

- These are warriors whose deepest desire is to hear Jesus welcome them with the following words when they enter into His presence:

> .... 'Well done, good and faithful servant. You have been faithful over a little; I will set you over much. Enter into the joy of your master.' *Matthew 25:21*

OPENING THE 6TH SEAL

------ ------ ------

A GREAT WAR IS COMING

(Revelation 6:12-17; Ezekiel 38 & 39)

SESSION #4 – WORKBOOK
Intended For
"KINGDOM WARRIORS IN THE ARMY OF GOD"

Unveiling Mysteries in the "Book of Revelation"

Based upon the Book:
GOD'S ANOINTED WARRIORS
By
Dr. Donald Bell
Major USMC, Ret.

(Slides # 2 - 8)

THE OPENING OF THE 6TH SEAL

> When he opened the sixth seal, I looked, and behold, there was **a great earthquake**, and the sun became black as sackcloth, the full moon became like blood, and the stars of the sky fell to the earth as the fig tree sheds its winter fruit when shaken by a gale. The sky vanished like a scroll that is being rolled up, and every mountain and island was removed from its place.
>
> Then the kings of the earth and the great ones and the generals and the rich and the powerful, and everyone, slave and free, hid themselves in the caves and among the rocks of the mountains, calling to the mountains and rocks, **"Fall on us and hide us from the face of him who is seated on the throne, and from the wrath of the Lamb,** for the great day of their wrath has come, and who can stand?" *Revelation 6:12-17*

Obviously this terrifying 6th seal event is yet future since nothing this extraordinary has occurred in human history since the time that John received this vision.

Key Points:

Observe those who are hiding themselves and trembling in fear of Almighty God and His Son, Jesus Christ whom they now recognize as the King of the universe.

- Many of them are the powerful ones of the world, strong in authority, who control the world's finances and dominate the social and political direction of mankind.

- They are also among those strong in wisdom – yet, people who have always denied the Christ in their worldly philosophies and who in their egotistical minds, ridiculed the people of the Lord who believe the message of the gospel.

However, this is not yet their end, for eventually this powerful group of worldly leaders, who are seen quaking in fear, will acclimate to this season of chaotic events and will organize, like ancient Babel, to fight against the Lord and His people.

- Only this time they will understand that they are aligning with the world and fighting against the almighty God of Christianity.

- Even though they now have no doubt that God is real, they will refuse to submit to Him. They plan to organize the entire world to fight against the Lord and His people.

Now in the past when significant disasters struck different nations of the world, the great majority of people did not see the hand of God in it, but simply assumed them to be natural disasters. But here they recognize that this great earthquake is from the Lord.

Okay, so what is it about this catastrophe that causes mankind to realize that it evolves from the wrath of God and is not simply a natural disaster?

- ➤ An obvious answer is that this sixth seal catastrophe is triggered by another event designed to strike at the heart of the Lord.
- ➤ A worldly event so massive and powerful against the Kingdom of God that only the Lord Himself could possibly bring about its defeat.

For Example:

- ➤ Approximately 3,500 years ago, the Lord brought ten plagues against Egypt, the most powerful nation in the known world and subsequently, drowned their mighty army in the Red Sea in the process of delivering His people from the world's bondage.

- ➤ This divine deliverance was known throughout all the Middle Eastern countries and they came to realize that the God of Israel was truly, the most powerful God, but they refused to submit to Him and give up their idolatrous lifestyle.

Although this awareness of God brought about a great fear upon these nations, nevertheless the great majority of them continued to oppose the people of God rather than unite with them.

Now a great event is about to take place that will grab the attention and concern of the entire world.

- ➤ An event that may possibly trigger the opening of the sixth seal as well as the subsequent trumpet judgments that we'll address in a future session.

Also it is very probable that there is a parallel connection between:
- ➤ The 6th seal event and the coming trumpet series.

Now let's look at a coming war that could well be the event that launches an era of great tribulation.

➤ A mighty army is about to descend upon the nation of Israel.

Notes:

_____
_____
_____
_____
_____
_____
_____

(Slides # 9 - 11)

A GREAT WAR BEGINS IN THE MIDDLE EAST
(Ezekiel 38 & 39)

Approximately 2600 years ago, the Lord spoke to his prophet Ezekiel **concerning a great army from the north that was going to descend upon the nation of Israel <u>in the "latter days</u>."**

The name "Gog" appears to be a title of the leader of these nations. Listen to the Lord speaking to the leader (Gog) of these nations who will come against Israel:

> After many days you will be mustered. <u>**In the latter years**</u> you will go against the land that is restored from war, the land whose people were gathered from many peoples upon the mountains of Israel, which had been a continual waste. Its people were brought out from the peoples and now dwell securely, all of them.
>
> <u>You will advance, coming on like a storm. You will be like a cloud covering the land, you and all your hordes, and many peoples with you.</u> **Ezekiel 38:8-9**

<u>Key Points:</u>

This is an army made up of a coalition of several nations, being led by one of the largest and most powerful nations in the world.

➢ Ezekiel was told that this attack would occur in the "latter days" when the inhabitants of Israel have been gathered from many nations and have resettled in the land.

Since 1948 Israel has been an established nation whose citizens of Jewish descent have been gathered from various other nations around the world.

➢ Now, Israel is quite a small nation with a population approximating seven million yet, it is also a prosperous nation that is well-armed and nuclear capable, thanks to the United States who, together with Great Britain, has been its chief ally since its formation sixty years ago.

➢ However, as a nation, the great majority of the Jewish people and their government are virtually secular and though they respect their ancient heritage, they have little concern for the Lord who, through their father Abraham, established them as a nation

<u>**Some folks may wonder then, why does God care for them as a nation?**</u>

Notes:
_____
_____
_____
_____

(Slides # 12 - 13)

OUR LORD'S UNCONDITIONAL COVENANT WITH ISRAEL

It goes back to His "Unconditional Covenant" over 4,000 years ago when He made the following promise to Abraham, the father of Israel:

> I will make of you a great nation, and I will bless you and make your name great, so that you will be a blessing. **I will bless those who bless you, and him who dishonors you I will curse**, and in you all the families of the earth shall be blessed." *Genesis 12:2-3*

However, that covenant was not made because the Lord holds Israel to be a righteous nation, for He says,

> And I will vindicate the holiness of my great name, which has been profaned among the nations, and **which you have profaned among them**.
>
> **And the nations will know that I am the Lord, declares the Lord God, when through you I vindicate my holiness before their eyes.** I will take you from the nations and gather you from all the countries and bring you into your own land. *Ezekiel 36:23-24*

(Slide # 14)

GOD'S HISTORICAL PURPOSE FOR ESTABLISHING ISRAEL

That through the Israelites and their testimony and/or their circumstances, <u>God will reveal Himself unto all the peoples of the earth.</u>

> **Now a "Great War" is about to be launched in the Middle East:**
>
> ➤ The Lord Himself will initiate this Great War by putting "hooks" into the jaws of the enemies of Israel and dragging them to a place where He will pour out His wrath to such an extent, that the entire world will tremble,
>
> ➤ And like the ancient Egyptians, they will come to realize that the Lord of Israel is surely the one true God. **Yet, the majority of peoples will continue to hate Him.**

Notes:
_____
_____
_____

BREAK-TIME (Slides # 15 - 16)

(Slides # 17 - 18)

A MIGHTY ARMY DESCENDS UPON ISRAEL

Now let's look at the nations that comprise this massive coalition that descends upon Israel with the intent to wipe out the Jewish race.

Key Points:

Modern day Russia, known as Magog in the bible is described as the leader of this "Axis of Evil" and Iran (Persia) is mentioned first among the countries that align with Russia.

A summary of the nations is as follows (Ezekiel 38:2-6):

1. Russia   2. Iran   3. Sudan   4. Ethiopia   5. Libya   6. Algeria

7. Tunisia   8. Turkey   9. Gomer = possibly Southeastern Europe

10. Many peoples with you = possibly Palestinians, Hezbollah, Hamas, ISIS

Note that these nations (with the exception of Russia) are mostly Islamic that have harbored a deep hatred for Israel since their formation as a nation.

➢ Ezekiel's description of this army suggests that it will be one of the largest and best equipped military forces ever assembled and by viewing their weaponry in modern terms, it appears to consist of a countless number of infantry troops & weaponry armed to the maximum.

➢ Ezekiel goes on to state that these powerful forces will advance on Israel like a "storm" and like a "cloud covering the land". This certainly sounds like a massive onslaught of ground and air forces.

Notes:

_____
_____
_____
_____
_____
_____
_____

ORACLE OF DAMASCUS
Isaiah 17:1

It is interesting to note that Syria who has historically been an enemy of Israel is not on the list;. One can surmise that this war will occur when Syria no longer has the military capability to join their allies in their mission to destroy the nation of Israel.

Key Points:

The absence of Syria presents a very interesting scenario for those who are familiar with "The Oracle of Damascus" where it was prophesized by Isaiah that a future time was coming when **"Damascus will cease to be a city and will become a "heap of ruins".** (Isa.17:1)

- This "Oracle of Damascus" goes on to describe the terror that will confront Israel and what will happen to their enemies. (Isaiah 17:12-14)

- Now, it may be that a war between Israel and Syria will **precede** the invasion of Israel by the military forces led by Russia and Iran.

- In fact, the destruction of Damascus and the defeat of the Syrian army may be the episode that ignites the Russian invasion of Israel.

- This could well be the "hook" in the Soviet's jaws that the Lord uses to draw them into the war for there currently exists a Syrian-Soviet treaty where Russia has pledged to provide military support in the event that Syria becomes engaged in battle with Israel over the Golan Heights.

Notes:

(Slide # 20)

RUSSIA'S MOTIVE FOR INVADING ISRAEL

Why would Russia be motivated to commit all of its forces to assist the Middle Eastern countries against their enemy, Israel?

<u>Key Points:</u>

Ezekiel tells us that Magog (Russia) desires <u>"to seize spoil and carry off plunder"</u>; which in our modern day makes a lot of sense since the Middle Eastern countries control the majority of oil resources which drive the world's economy.

➢ Russia definitely wants to regain its super-power status among the nations of the world and this alliance with the Middle Eastern nations may be an opportunity to unseat the United States as being the strongest and most influential political and economic power in the world.

➢ Now comes an opportunity to become the greatest and wealthiest nation on earth – this is definitely a "hook" that the Lord could use to draw Russia into this devastating conflict.

Iran's goals for the war are certainly different than Russia's, so why would Iran and other Middle Eastern countries welcome Russian support in their mission to wipe out Israel from the face of the world?

➢ Because Russia possesses the military capability and technology that these countries need in order to subdue Israel. The Islamic nations have warred against Israel since its formation and have met with hardly any success. **They need military help**.

Notes:

(Slide # 21)

THE UNITED STATES WILL ABANDON IT'S SUPPORT OF ISRAEL

In his prophecy, Ezekiel rules out the possibility that any country will come to Israel's defense once Russia and Iran and their allies launch their invasion from the north.

Key Points:

So what is it that will cause our country to abandon its support for Israel at the moment of their greatest crisis?

- Obviously, the United States of today is a politically divided country. As Americans tire more and more of our Middle Eastern conflicts, the leftist voices grow louder in their support of a Palestinian State with no concern for the consequences to Israel.

- It is most probable that this war will occur when America is completely governed by leftist Democrats; a government that may decry an invasion of Israel, but would not militarily attempt to stop it.

- Ezekiel's prophecy indicates that there will be a verbal protest from Saudi Arabia and nations in the west (Tarshish) but obviously, they will not lift a hand to interfere.[10]

It is obvious that without the intervention of the United States or a united Europe (which is becoming very anti-Semitic), there is no one else on the planet who could possibly stand against these tremendous forces that will soon be mustered against the nation of Israel.

In short, the kingdom of this world hates the nation of Israel and its citizenry wherever they are living; **but in reality, it is a hatred for the God of Israel.**

For Israel, even though it is primarily a secular culture, is still the nation that God uses to make His name known throughout the world:

> "And my holy name I will make known in the midst of my people Israel, and I will not let my holy name be profaned anymore. **And the nations shall know that I am the Lord, the Holy One in Israel."** *Ezekiel 39:7*

Notes:

___

[10] Ezekiel 38:13

(Slides # 22 - 23)

THE INVASION FROM THE NORTH AND
THE LORD'S RESPONSE

Ezekiel's prophecy reports that this military alliance will descend toward the mountains known today as the Golan Heights, which is Israel's northern border adjacent to Syria, Lebanon, and northern Jordan.

Ezekiel describes the following devastations that will be poured out upon these enemies of Israel when they reach the Golan Heights:

Ezekiel 38:18-23

But on that day, the day that Gog shall come against the land of Israel, declares the Lord God, my wrath will be roused in my anger. For in my jealousy and in my blazing wrath I declare,
On that day there shall be a great earthquake in the land of Israel.

➢ The fish of the sea and the birds of the heavens and the beasts of the field and all creeping things that creep on the ground, and all the people who are on the face of the earth, shall quake at my presence.

➢ And the mountains shall be thrown down, and the cliffs shall fall, and every wall shall tumble to the ground.

➢ I will summon a sword against Gog on all my mountains, declares the Lord God. Every man's sword will be against his brother.

➢ With pestilence and bloodshed I will enter into judgment with him, and

➢ I will rain upon him and his hordes and the many peoples who are with him torrential rains and hailstones, fire and sulfur.

So I will show my greatness and my holiness and make myself known in the eyes of many nations. Then they will know that I am the Lord.

Such a shaking of the earth has never yet occurred throughout the history of mankind.

Notes:
_____
_____
_____
_____
_____

(Slide # 24)

THE INVASION FROM THE NORTH AND THE LORD'S RESPONSE - SUMMARY

Note: The "great earthquake" described in this war may be the same "earthquake" that strikes the earth when the Lord opens the "sixth seal".

To Summarize these devastations:

- The mountains and cliffs fall upon this invading army (Sounds like avalanches).
- Hailstones, fire, and sulfur rain down upon their heads.
- Deadly diseases sweep through their ranks
- Tremendous panic and confusion will eliminate discipline among the troops and they will begin to fire their weapons against one another causing a great massacre within their own ranks.
- This sudden devastation is so great that all the nations of the earth, will quake at the presence of the Lord as His fury is poured out on the armies of the enemies of His people.

When this occurs, there will no longer be any doubt that the God of Israel and Christianity is the one and true God.

Key Points:

This is a similar scenario to that ancient time when God delivered His people from Egypt and provided safe passage through the Red Sea and then, He wiped out the entire Egyptian army which was, in that period of history, the most powerful military force in the world.

- All the nations of that day knew that the God of Israel was God; but, this event will be so much more catastrophic.
- All the nations shall know that the God of Israel is the Lord and will not allow His name to be profaned anymore.
- That doesn't mean that they won't hate Him, but they certainly will be more careful in their future plans for world domination.

Notes:

(Slide # 25)

A TIME OF CLEANSING OF THE LAND

Following the earthquake and the devastation that took place on the Golan Heights, the people of Israel who are unharmed will go out to clean up the land where they will gather all the wreckage of the weaponry for burning.

Key Points:

- It will take seven years of constant fires to cleanse the land of the residue of the planes, helicopters, artillery, tanks, trucks, jeeps, trailers, small arms, supplies, and all other equipment that is destroyed.

- The birds of the air and the beasts of the field will eat the flesh of this once mighty army and drink the blood of those previously considered "princes of the earth."

- As for the remaining carcasses, we are told that all the people of the land of Israel would assist in burying the bodies in a massive graveyard east of the Dead Sea. Even though the entire population of Israel will be locating and transporting the bodies to this burial site, it will be seven months before the land will be completely clean of all the carcasses.

- The former leader of this army, identified as Gog will also be buried. Gog is not a personal name, but more likely a title like prince, or czar, or president, or general. The burial site will be called the Valley of Hamon-Gog.

- It appears as if hundreds of thousands will be killed during this coming day when the Lord magnifies His holiness as a Defender of His people in Israel.

Now - all the peoples of Israel shall know that the God of Abraham, Isaac, and Jacob, is truly their God who stands against their enemies.

This great earthquake will be the most catastrophic, worldwide event ever witnessed by mankind since the flood, but the end is not yet; events are about to intensify.

Notes:

BREAK-TIME (Slides # 25 - 27)

(Slides # 28 - 29)

CATASTROPHIC EVENTS WILL FOLLOW THIS WAR

There is another very significant event that takes place following the devastation resulting from this great earthquake. The Lord is not yet done, for Ezekiel receives this additional prophecy from the God of Israel.

> I will send **fire** on **Magog** and on those who dwell securely in the **coastlands**, and they shall know that I am the Lord. *Ezekiel 39:6*

This implies a sending of "fire" upon two groups of people - Russia and those on the coastlands. **Sounds very much like a <u>nuclear war</u>**.

Two Possible Scenarios to Consider:

First - World-Wide Nuclear War:

➤ When God's earthquake hits Israel, fear, confusion, and chaos will cause exchanges of fire within the Russian forces. Escalation will ensue and the Russians may well think that the west is attacking them. It is possible that a nuclear exchange will begin inadvertently.

➤ Ezekiel does not identify the people inhabiting the "coastlands in security"; but he does say they will also be on the receiving end of this nuclear war. The United States is the only nation capable of engaging the Soviets in a major nuclear war and thus, it's possible that Russia may launch the first strike against the west who will then retaliate.

Second – Coordinated Islamic Acts of Terrorism

The Muslim world has been anxiously waiting 1,200 years for the coming of their messiah, known as the Mahdi.

Now the chief sign which announces the coming of their Islamic messiah is a "massive earthquake" which is intended to launch a global war to kill and/or to subjugate Jews, Christians, and other "infidels."

➤ This Islamic belief may very well cause them to launch an internal nuclear attack on various cities in the western world following the great earthquake that the Lord releases in the Golan Heights believing that this will initiate the return of their Mahdi messiah.

➤ Also, these Muslim terrorists on both the western and eastern continents could possibly detonate nuclear "suitcase bombs" in various cities in retaliation for what they see is an attack upon the Middle Eastern world.

This catastrophic effect of a probable nuclear attack may be what John describes in greater detail in the series known as "the seven trumpets which destroy 1/3 of the world".

(Slides # 30 - 33)

A PROBABLE NUCLEAR WAR – THE 6TH SEAL

Now, nuclear weapons were initially produced in our country for the purpose of protecting our freedoms. However today, they are also considered to be of great importance to an evil segment of mankind who desire worldly control.

Throughout history, God has used various nations to bring judgment on those nations who have forsaken Him or have done great evil against His people. This appears to be a judgment from God, as the 6th seal is opened - yet it is not the final judgment.

This is a war that God allows man to bring upon himself AND this is a war that will end national sovereignty among the nations and bring about a New World Order

---

Key Points:

The Probability Of A Nuclear War Being Launched By The Opening Of The 6th Seal.

The Great Earthquake
- It is probably the same earthquake that launches the destruction of the invading army from the north on the Golan Heights.

The sun becomes black as sackcloth & the moon becomes like blood
- This appears to be the result of the detonation of hundreds of nuclear warheads that will cause smoke to be launched into the atmosphere resulting in a miles-think, dark curtain throughout the skies.

The stars fell to the earth as a fig tree sheds its winter fruit when shaken by a gale
- Nuclear hail is formed when large quantities of earth and water are sucked into the fireball and become vaporized.
- Subsequently, they gradually descend to the earth in what we call "fallout." At first, this fallout is generally the size of marbles, but over time - lighter particles continue to fall like dusty snow.
- However, - this could also be a vision of a fiery streak of rocket exhaust from nuclear tipped missiles as they sour through the atmosphere.

The sky vanished like a scroll that is being rolled up
- A nuclear detonation will result in strong updrafts just seconds after the explosion. It then rises several miles into a darkening sky.
- Eventually, a gigantic mushroom shaped cloud is formed which gives the visual impression of the "sky vanishing like a scroll that is being rolled up.

It is possible that this catastrophic effect of a probable nuclear attack may be what the apostle John describes in greater detail in the series known as "the seven trumpets which destroy 1/3 of the world".

BREAK-TIME   **(Slides # 34 - 35)**

(Slide # 36)

THE GOG MAGOG WAR – A SECOND ONE COMING?

The Book of Revelation does speak of another Gog Magog war that occurs at the end of time.[11]

> Key Points:
>
> However, this is a second war that is yet further into the future, not this war that is recorded by Ezekiel. We know this for several reasons:
>
> 1. First, Ezekiel's war occurs relatively soon after the rebirth of the nation of Israel and the ingathering of the Jewish people from around the world. <u>The second Gog Magog war occurs after Jesus has reigned on earth for 1,000 years.</u>
>
> 2. Second, Ezekiel's war involves a fearsome, but limited coalition of countries that surround Israel. <u>The war in Revelation involves all the nations from "every corner of the earth" coming to attack Israel.</u>
>
> 3. Finally, after Ezekiel's war, life continues; bodies are gathered and buried for seven months; weaponry is gathered and burned for seven years. By contrast, <u>the war in Revelation is followed immediately by the end of this world and the coming of a new heaven and earth.</u> (This scenario will also will be addressed in a subsequent session)

(Slide # 37)

SUMMARY OF EVENTS CONCERNING WORLD-WIDE WARFARE

This Great War in Ezekiel 38 & 39 triggers an earthquake that may be the same earthquake in the 6th seal event.

➢ This earthquake, together with other catastrophic events destroy a mighty army and all those who survive do know that it was the God of Abraham, Isaac, & Jacob that intervened and defeated the enemies of His chosen people.

➢ Yet, most of those who are seen trembling in fear of God will later arise to establish a one-world government much like ancient Babel, with the objective of wiping out the people of God from the face of the earth. However, following this war, they will make a seven-year covenant with the nation of Israel which they will break after 3 ½ years.

➢ Following this earthquake and the Middle Eastern War, there is an exchange of "fire" upon two groups of people - Russia and those on the coastlands.

It is highly probable that this is a nuclear war which is more specifically revealed in the coming judgments known as the "Seven Trumpets."

---

[11] Revelation 20:7-10

(Slides # 38 - 41)

WORLD WAR AND THE CHRISTIAN ATTITUDE

True followers of Jesus Christ may be the only friends Israel and the Jewish people will have left as this terrible war approaches.

- The Jews in America will undoubtedly be maligned & persecuted during this scheme of events. We must, with all of our heart, align ourselves with them and show our solidarity for their people and their nation.

- At the same time, we must remember that God loves the Muslim people of the Middle East as well as the Russians and others living in the former Soviet Union.

- Lovers of Christ must love and show compassion to all people. This doesn't mean excusing the actions of anti-Christian governments, **but it is believer's hard work to demonstrate and communicate Christ's love during mankind's darkest hours.** [12]

Jesus Christ is the one and only way to eternal life, and those who receive Him as their eternal Savior, are redeemed by this precious blood of the "Lamb of God"------- He is also the "Lion of Judah." He is so mighty and powerful, yet possesses such a deep love for His people, that it is just incomprehensible.[13]

Notes:

_____
_____
_____
_____
_____

---

[12] Joel C. Rosenberg, *Epicenter : why the current rumblings in the Middle East will change your future,* (Tyndale House Publishers, Inc., 2006) p. 250
[13] Revelation 1:12-18; Daniel 10:5-12

(Slide # 42)

THE NEXT SESSION:

First Read: Revelation 7

An Interlude that Precedes the Trumpet Judgments

GOD'S END-TIME WARRIORS = 144,000

- 144,000 "Servants = Army of God in the Last Days
- Who are the Sons of Israel Reflected by the Twelve Tribes?
- A Brief History of the Northern Kingdom of Israel
- Israel (Ephraim) Now Living Among the Nations
- Is America home to the descendants of Ephraim
- The Meaning of the Number "144,000"
- The Identity of the 144,000 Sealed Servants of God
- A Numberless Multitude Worshipping Before the Throne
- Leadership Qualities that Identify the "144,000"

Additional Notes:

THE LAMB OF GOD - OUR TRUE "COMMANDER-IN-CHIEF"

The days are rapidly approaching when a tremendous separation will take place among mankind.

Yet, during this present era of warfare, He reigns as our Commander-in-Chief and His Name continues to be the battle cry for those warriors who fight daily for righteousness and truth.

His name is Jesus, Our Lord, Our King, Our Commander-in-Chief

- A truly mighty Leader who would never delegate assignments to His people that He Himself wouldn't readily embrace.

- A Commander that Christian warriors will readily follow not matter the danger or what costs have to be paid.

- These are warriors whose deepest desire is to hear Jesus welcome them with the following words when they enter into His presence:

.... 'Well done, good and faithful servant. You have been faithful over a little; I will set you over much. Enter into the joy of your master.' *Matthew 25:21*

GOD'S END-TIME WARRIORS
= = = = = = = =
"144,000"

(Revelation 7)

SESSION #5 – WORKBOOK
Intended For
"KINGDOM WARRIORS IN THE ARMY OF GOD"

Unveiling Mysteries in the "Book of Revelation"

Based upon the Book:
GOD'S ANOINTED WARRIORS
By
Dr. Donald Bell
Major USMC, Ret.

(Slides # 2 - 4)

SUMMARY OF THE FIRST SIX SEALS

Recall that the breaking of the first five seals began in the 1st century shortly after the gospel of Jesus Christ first went out into the world.

➢ These spiritual powers, symbolized by the four horsemen, continue to affect the entire world. Yet Jesus refers to these afflictions as "merely the beginning of birth pains."

Now the tremendously devastating event that is launched with the opening of the 6th seal has not yet occurred.

➢ However, it is highly probable that the 6th seal "earthquake" that rocks the world is the same earthquake described in book of Ezekiel when a mighty army from the north descends upon the nation of Israel and destroyed on the Golan Heights.

➢ It is also probable that this massive earthquake is the trigger that will launch a global nuclear war which will devastate 1/3 of the entire earth. This is depicted in the forthcoming trumpet series which will be addressed in the next session.

Thus, what we see in the opening of the 6th seal is a portrayal of the entire scenario beginning with a great earthquake and evolving into a nuclear holocaust.

➢ All of this is extremely hard for Christians to accept as a forthcoming event is allowed by the Lord Himself - but we must remember that this will also be a time of opportunity to stand and fight for the Kingdom of God against a spiritual enemy that will soon launch the most powerful offensive attack against the church since the beginning of time.

➢ The Lord is calling us to join Him in this great end-time war against the forces of the Prince of Darkness who has kept mankind in bondage for the last 6,000 years.

Notes:
_____
_____
_____
_____
_____
_____
_____

(Slides # 5 - 6)

HOPE CONTINUES TO SHINE IN THE MIDST OF DARKNESS

Tremendous devastation will take place on the earth during the coming period of "trumpet judgments." One-third of the earth, the seas, and mankind are targeted for destruction, yet two-thirds will survive.

Key Points:

However, if it were God's purpose to destroy the entire earth, He wouldn't do it in stages.

➢ These trumpet judgments are unbelievably devastating, yet they are still warnings to mankind and a **call for repentance**.

In fact, God will plant His chosen warriors among the nations to be powerfully anointed ministers for Christ during this time of great suffering.

➢ For before the first trumpet sounds, the Lord will send an angel to seal His "servants of God" in order to prepare them for the trumpet judgments that will soon descend upon the earth.

Then I saw another angel ascending from the rising of the sun, with the seal of the living God, and he called with a loud voice to the four angels who had been given power to harm earth and sea, saying, "Do not harm the earth or the sea or the trees, until we have sealed the **servants** of our God on their foreheads." And I heard the number of the sealed, **144,000, sealed from every tribe of the sons of Israel:** *Revelation 7:2-4*

(Slide # 7)

"144,000" SERVANTS = ARMY OF GOD IN LAST DAYS

<u>"Servants"</u> is an English word that really doesn't fully communicate the character of these men and women who will receive the seal of God prior to the launching of the trumpet series of events.

➢ In both Hebrew and Greek - it is a description applied to the apostles, to the prophets, to Moses, to the true worshippers of Christ,[14] and to anyone who gives himself wholly to another without regard to personal interests.[15]

➢ These are the characteristics found in these mighty "servants of God."

<u>Key Points:</u>

This group of 144,000 are warrior-spirited servants serving as soldiers in the Army of God during the latter days.

➢ They are totally sold out to the Lord Jesus Christ and will glorify His name with their lives throughout the latter days of God's judgments.

➢ They are the God's Anointed Warriors in the Body of Christ whose light will continue to shine in the midst of great darkness.

➢ They will bring the hope of salvation to millions of people who are scared and searching for answers.

These <u>"warrior-spirited servants of God"</u> are commonly known as the 144,000 Sons of Israel descended from the twelve tribes of Israel.

➢ They represent "God's Anointed Warriors" that are the disciples who will be empowered and dispatched by their King, Jesus Christ to minister in the midst of the Great Tribulation.

Notes:

_____
_____
_____
_____

---

[14] Acts 10:36; Ephesians 6:6
[15] 1 Corinthians 7:23

(Slide # 8)

WHO ARE THE "SONS OF ISRAEL" REFLECTED BY THE 12 TRIBES?

> **And I heard the number of the sealed, 144,000, sealed from every tribe of the sons of Israel:**
>
> | | |
> |---|---|
> | 12,000 from the tribe of **Judah** = Jews | 12,000 from the tribe of Reuben, |
> | 12,000 from the tribe of Gad, | 12,000 from the tribe of Asher, |
> | 12,000 from the tribe of Naphtali, | 12,000 from the tribe of Manasseh, |
> | 12,000 from the tribe of **Simeon** = Jews | 12,000 from the tribe of Levi, |
> | 12,000 from the tribe of Issachar, | 12,000 from the tribe of Zebulun, |
> | 12,000 from the tribe of Joseph, (Ephraim) | 12,000 from the tribe of **Benjamin** = Jews |
>
> *Revelation 7:4-8*

Before discussing their identity in our generation, understand that there are primarily two opposing views which are widely held by the western church:

First, there is what many call the "pre-tribulation dispensational" view.

Adherents of this view believe that the 12 tribes of Israel who are sealed prior to the trumpet series are the latter day Jewish people from the nation of Israel.

➤ This view teaches that only Jewish people will comprise the earthly church during the Great Tribulation since the present day Christian church will have been raptured.

Additionally, they also "assume" that natural Israel is simply today's "Jews."

➤ This view erroneously infers that since the descendants of the northern tribes (who are not Jewish) can no longer be visibly identified, they cannot be counted among the sons of Israel.

Second, there is what is commonly known as the "spiritual Israel" view.

Adherents of this view believe that these 12 tribes of Israel represent the New Testament church.

➤ This teaching that the church has replaced Israel as the chosen people of God is commonly called **"replacement theology"** and has been embraced by many in the church for centuries.

➤ Now, there certainly are some New Testament verses which address the parallelism between Israel and the Church.[16] Yet these passages do not teach that the Israelite nation has been replaced by the church as God's New Testament people.

➤ This is a false theology and a very dangerous teaching that resulted in hatred toward the Jews whose descendants are continually blamed for the crucifixion of Christ.

---

[16] Galatians 3:29; Philippians 3:3; Romans 2:28-29; 9:6

Notes:

(Slide # 9)

WHO ARE THE "SONS OF ISRAEL" REFLECTED BY THE 12 TRIBES?

Now this brings us to another perspective that is much more rational and biblically sound than those teachings outlined above.

<u>First - Note the following question:</u>

➢ Why are all "twelve tribes" of Israel included among those sealed prior to the trumpet judgments?"

And I heard the number of the sealed, 144,000, sealed from every tribe of the sons of Israel:	
12,000 from the tribe of **<u>Judah</u>** = Jews	12,000 from the tribe of Reuben,
12,000 from the tribe of Gad,	12,000 from the tribe of Asher,
12,000 from the tribe of Naphtali,	12,000 from the tribe of Manasseh,
12,000 from the tribe of **<u>Simeon</u>** = Jews	12,000 from the tribe of Levi,
12,000 from the tribe of Issachar,	12,000 from the tribe of Zebulun,
12,000 from the tribe of Joseph, (Ephraim)	12,000 from the tribe of **<u>Benjamin</u>** = Jews

Revelation 7:4-8

Key Points:

Today's Jews are descendants of only a couple of tribes, primarily Judah & Benjamin, which historically comprised the Southern Kingdom of Israel known as the Judeans.

➢ However, this sealing of 144,000 also includes tribes within the Northern Kingdom of Israel which were scattered among the nations of the world over 2,700 years ago.

➢ Thus, the identity of the 144,000 runs much deeper than those traditional views of modern day theologians who erroneously teach that either all Israel means "the church" or "the Jews".

➢ Let's take a look; perhaps you will find the following both intriguing and enlightening.

Notes:

___
___
___
___
___

(Slide # 10)

A BRIEF HISTORY OF THE NORTHERN KINGDOM OF ISRAEL

The Bible records that the foolishness of King Rehoboam, who was the son of Solomon, caused the Northern Tribes to rebel and establish a separate nation.

This occurred around 930 BC, when Israel was divided into two separate kingdoms.

Tribes in the Northern Kingdom of Israel = Israelites or Ephraimites					
1. Reuben	2. Gad	3. Asher	4. Naphtali	5. Manasseh	
6. Issachar	7. Ephraim	8. Zebulun	9. Levi (partial)	10. Dan	

Tribes in the Southern Kingdom of Judah = Jews			
1. Judah	2. Benjamin	3. Simeon	4. Levi (partial)

However, a small number of peoples among the northern tribes did later emigrate to the south.

Now let's take a brief look at what happened to both these northern and southern tribes following their division into two separate kingdoms:

Over a period of 200 plus years, 19 "evil kings", ruled over the **Northern Kingdom**, which evolved into a tremendously dark and idolatrous nation. After they continually refused to listen to the prophetic messengers that the Lord sent to them, the nation of Assyria, an enemy of Israel, was commissioned by God to conquer the Northern Kingdom in 722 BC. It was a brutal massacre of men, women, and children, but those who survived were all deported from the land and forced to assimilate into other nations and cultures where they completely lost their religious and national identity. Thus, the Northern Kingdom of Israel was gone and these 10 Tribes never reappeared in the pages of history after their defeat by the Assyrians.

The **Southern Kingdom** continued to remain in the land, although 130 years later, due to their idolatrous lifestyle, they were conquered by the Babylonians and went into captivity for 70 years (beginning in 605 BC) after which approximately 50,000 people returned to their homeland and the city of Jerusalem. These 50,000 who chose to leave Babylon (536 BC) and return to their country are those who came to be known as the "Jews". Yet, as many as 95% of the Judean descendants chose to remain in Babylon and were assimilated into the Babylonian culture.

Why is this important?

➢ **It gives us understanding of where today's "Jews" come from.**

➢ **This means that the descendants of the Northern Tribes, as well as those who remained in Babylon, are "not" considered "Jews."**

BREAK-TIME (Slides # 11 - 12)

(Slide # 13)

GOD'S COVENANT EMBRACES ALL THE DESCENDANTS OF ISRAEL

Isn't it somewhat ironic that today's "Jews" are continually referred to as national Israel, yet they represent a very, very, small fraction of Abraham's descendants through Isaac and Jacob?

Now this does raise some interesting questions:
- Didn't God make His covenant with "all" the descendants of Abraham, Isaac, and Jacob which are represented by the 12 tribes of Israel?

In fact – they were to be become a multitude of nations:

Genesis 17:3-7

> And God said to him, "Behold, my covenant is with you, and **you shall be the father of a multitude of nations.**
> No longer shall your name be called Abram, but your name shall be Abraham, **for I have made you the father of a multitude of nations.**
> I will make you exceedingly fruitful, and **I will make you into nations**, and kings shall come from you. **And I will establish my covenant between me and you and your offspring after you throughout their generations for an everlasting covenant, to be God to you and to your offspring after you.**

Because of the disappearance of the Northern Tribes, does this covenant now apply only to the house of Judah? Consider the following:

- **Just before the fall of the Northern Kingdom in 722 BC, the Lord sent the prophet Hosea to Israel to prophesy concerning the coming captivity.**

> In order to illustrate His long-suffering nature for Ephraim, the Lord told his chosen prophet, Hosea to marry a harlot. Subsequently, she was unfaithful to Hosea which broke his heart and she left him for other lovers. After a period of time, the Lord told Hosea to forgive her and take her back and be restored as his wife. Likewise, the Lord states that Ephraim would someday be restored and become His Bride. [17]

In his writings, Hosea foretold what was to take place for Ephraim (10 Northern Tribes) after their disappearance into captivity – that is:

- The number of their descendants would be more than the "sand of the sea which cannot be measured." [18]
- They were to be rejected and become "wanderers among the nations." [19]
- However, the Lord was not finished with the Northern Tribes, nor would He ever be finished with them. [20]

---

[17] Hosea 2:14-23; Zechariah 10:6
[18] Hosea 1:10
[19] Hosea 7:8, 8:8, 9:17; Micah 5:7-8
[20] Hosea 11:8-9

(Slide # 14)

GOD'S COVENANT EMBRACES ALL THE DESCENDANTS OF ISRAEL

Hosea foretold what was to take place for the 10 Northern Tribes after their disappearance into captivity – that is:

1. The number of their descendants would be more than the "sand of the sea which cannot be measured."

2. They would become "wanderers among the nations."

3. The Lord was not finished with the Northern Tribes, nor would He ever be finished with them.

4. Ephraim would someday be restored and become His Bride.

(Slide # 15)

ISRAEL (EPHRAIM) NOW LIVING AMONG THE NATIONS

4,000 years ago, Jacob laid his hands upon his grandson Ephraim (a son of Joseph) and prophesized that the descendants of Ephraim would become a multitude of nations.[21]

- As most bible scholars know, the name of Ephraim in scripture frequently refers to the entire Northern Kingdom.

- Certainly, Ephraim was the largest tribe, but as big as it got, it never became a multitude of nations before it disappeared in 722 BC.

- Well then, if it didn't happen before the disappearance, then Ephraim must have become a multitude of nations after its disappearance.

Not only will the descendants of Ephraim (Northern Kingdom) suddenly reappear, but after thousands of years of separation, they would once again be united with Judah (Southern Kingdom).[22]

- The prophet Ezekiel speaks clearly of this future uniting of Judah and Ephraim and we also learn from scripture **that when Ephraim returns back in the land of Israel where they were once cast out, they will be forever called "sons of the Living God."** [23]

---

[21] Genesis 48:19
[22] Larry Simmons, 42 Months to Glory (Oklahoma City, OK: Ephraim House Publishers, 1994), p.86
[23] Ezekiel 37:19-21; Hosea 1:10

(Slides # 16 - 19)

ISRAEL (EPHRAIM) NOW LIVING AMONG THE NATIONS

Now, approximately 150 years after the 10 northern tribes fell into captivity, the prophet Jeremiah revealed that God was going to make a New Covenant with the house of Judah "<u>and</u>" with the house of Israel?

> "Behold, the days are coming, declares the Lord, when <u>I will make a new covenant with the house of Israel and the house of Judah,</u> ……. But this is the covenant that I will make with the house of Israel after those days, declares the Lord: I will put my law within them, and I will write it on their hearts. And I will be their God, and they shall be my people. *Jeremiah 31:31 & 33*

Were the prophets mistaken when they heard from the Lord that He was going to forgive and restore (not replace) the house of Israel as a people of God?

> "<u>I will strengthen the house of Judah, and I will save the house of Joseph. I will bring them back because I have compassion on them, and they shall be as though I had not rejected them,</u> for I am the Lord their God and I will answer them. **Then Ephraim shall become like a mighty warrior, and their hearts shall be glad as with wine.** Their children shall see it and be glad; their hearts shall rejoice in the Lord. "I will whistle for them and gather them in, for I have redeemed them, and they shall be as many as they were before. **Though I scattered them among the nations, yet in far countries they shall remember me, and with their children they shall live and return.** *Zechariah 10:6-9*

There are numerous biblical prophecies predicting the restoration and uniting of the 12 tribes into one nation once again who will eternally serve the God of Abraham, Isaac, and Jacob.[24]
<u>One last example</u> – The Lord spoke the following to His prophet Ezekiel:

> "Son of man, take a stick and write on it, **'For Judah,** and the people of Israel associated with him'; then take another stick and write on it, **'For Joseph** (the stick of Ephraim) and all the house of Israel associated with him.' <u>And join them one to another into one stick,</u> that they may become one in your hand.
>
> And when your people say to you, 'Will you not tell us what you mean by these?' say to them, Thus says the Lord God: Behold, <u>I am about to take the stick of Joseph (that is in the hand of Ephraim) and the tribes of Israel associated with him. And I will join with it the stick of Judah, and make them one stick, that they may be one in my hand.</u>
>
> When the sticks on which you write are in your hand before their eyes, then say to them, Thus says the Lord God: <u>Behold, I will take the people of Israel from the nations among which they have gone, and will gather them from all around, and bring them to their own land. And I will make them one nation in the land, on the mountains of Israel. And one king shall be king over them all, and they shall be no longer two nations, and no longer divided into two kingdoms.</u> *Ezekiel 37:16-22*

---

[24] Hosea 11:8-9; Zechariah 10:6; Ezekiel 37: 16-22; Micah 5:7-8

(Slide # 20)

Now, it is true that descendants of the former northern tribes no longer exist as a single nation, yet they do exist worldwide in many nations.

- God has scattered them among the nations, but He is about to anoint and seal many of them for a future purpose.

- <u>**Well, where are they? Where has the Lord hidden them? Obviously, they don't even know themselves**</u>.

The fact that we have lost track of these descendants of the Northern Kingdom is irrelevant. Our Lord has made promises to those people which will be kept.

Notes:
_____
_____
_____
_____

(Slides # 21 - 22)

IS AMERICA - HOME TO THE DESCENDANTS OF EPHRAIM ?

<u>Well, let's take a look at where these descendants of Ephraim may currently live.</u>

➢ There are many stories concerning how numerous descendants of the 10 Lost Tribes have migrated to Europe.
➢ Also, it is interesting to note that the prophet <u>Hosea says that at the time of Ephraim's return to the land of Israel, many will come from "the west"</u>.[25]
➢ Certainly many of these peoples would have migrated into Europe and subsequently, to America.

It is a strong probability that a great number of the descendants of Ephraim are Christians living in the United States. <u>Note the following interesting parallels:</u>

<u>The Lord has put His laws on their hearts:</u>

➢ The covenant of circumcision was required of ancient Israel. Up until the 1980's, babies were routinely circumcised in the United States and millions still are today. This was one of the few nations upon earth, besides Israel, to do so. **Why us?**

➢ The United States was the first nation to have a five day work week, thus observing the Sabbath as well as Sunday. **Where did that originate?**

Finally, Paul tells us in Romans that "all Israel will be saved" when the "fullness of the Gentiles has come in." [26] **Perhaps this is because the "10 Northern Tribes" are mixed in with the Gentile nations.**

<u>Think about this!</u>
➢ When we consider our own genealogy, can we trace our roots back 200 years? 500 years? How about 2,700 years?

➢ Modern Israel consists of Jewish immigrants from many nations. Ephraim, with many more people and an 800 year head start, would be much more widespread than Judah.

➢ So, whether one is Hispanic, Asian, Negro, Indian, or Caucasian, it's more than probable that many of us are physical brothers and sisters descended from Abraham who have immigrated to many countries around the world. Only God knows with certainty.

➢ Now, this doesn't mean that every Christian is a descendant from Ephraim, although certainly many are; perhaps the great majority. But, like Rahab, Ruth, and Jethro, many Gentiles are also grafted into the promises of Israel.

BREAK-TIME **(Slides # 23 - 24)**

---

[25] Hosea 11:10
[26] Romans 11:25-27

(Slide # 25)

THE MEANING OF THE NUMBER "144,000"

Key Points:

The number twelve in the bible frequently represents the people of God. For example:

- 12 Tribes of Israel in the Old Testament

- 12 Apostles of Christ in the New Testament

- The 24 Elders before the throne of God in Revelation 4 are probably, representatives of God's people from both the Old Testament and the New Testament.

- The New Jerusalem will have 12 gates bearing the names of the 12 tribes of Israel and will also have 12 foundation stones bearing the names of the 12 Apostles.

- 144,000 will be sealed with the names of both the Father and the Son written on their foreheads.[27]

144,000 = 12 x 12 x 1,000.

- The use of the number 144,000 does not necessarily imply an exact number of those sealed; it is possibly symbolic of a perfect totality of those God has chosen to be sealed as His anointed witnesses prior to the coming trumpet series.

Notes:

---

[27] Revelation 14:1

(Slides # 26 - 27)

THE IDENTITY OF THE 144,000 SEALED SERVANTS OF GOD

> Key Points:
>
> **Who are the 144,000 sealed servants of God and where do they come from?**
>
> ➢ They are Christians descended from the tribes of the southern kingdom (Jews), <u>and</u>
>
> ➢ They are Christians descended from the tribes of the northern kingdom (Israelites or sons of Ephraim), <u>and</u>
>
> ➢ They are Christians descended from the gentile nations who have been grafted into God's people.
>
> **Currently, they reside in every nation around the world, but a day is coming when they will all gather together with their Commander-in-Chief, Jesus Christ on Mt. Zion.**[28]

The 144,000 who are sealed are a remnant of the church, not the whole.

➢ These are the mighty warriors in the Army of God who will lead His people during the reign of terror that will descend upon the earth; men and women who heard and obeyed the command of Jesus to "be prepared" for His coming.

➢ **These are the ones who choose to follow the Lamb wherever he goes and they are redeemed from mankind as "firstfruits for God and the Lamb.**[29]

This section of prophecy is not speaking of eternal salvation; it is an anointing of discipleship for those who will be a powerful light in the midst of the darkest period in the history of the world.

> Arise, shine, for your light has come, and the glory of the Lord has risen upon you.
> For behold, darkness shall cover the earth, and thick darkness the peoples; but the Lord will arise upon you, and his glory will be seen upon you. *Isaiah 60:1-2*

Many will be eternally saved but not sealed.

➢ We see a sign of this immediately after the sealing of the 144,000, when John is shown a numberless multitude from every nation worshipping before the throne of God.

---

[28] Revelation 14:1-5
[29] Revelation 14:4

(Slides # 28 - 29)

A NUMBERLESS MULTITUDE WORSHIPPING BEFORE THE THRONE
(Revelation 7:9-17)

This great multitude will be comprised of those Christians who were within the church at the launching of the latter day judgments as well as many others who are among the great harvest that will take place within the midst of the great tribulation.

These are Christians who have suffered tremendous sorrow, grief, hunger, and of course, persecution from the worldly system, but refused to compromise their faith even unto death.

Key Points:

This is a depiction of those who are now experiencing His glory, following their suffering and death in the midst of the great tribulation.

- Now they will reign forever and ever with our Lord because they have truly repented and were reborn into the kingdom of God.

- Death may be a blessing conferred on people for their faithfulness and to deliver them from evil times.

They are those who overcame the world like the Apostle Paul who believed that:

- *The Spirit himself bears witness with our spirit that we are children of God, and if children, then heirs-heirs of God and fellow heirs with Christ, provided we suffer with him in order that we may also be glorified with him. For I consider that the sufferings of this present time are not worth comparing with the glory that is to be revealed to us.* **Romans 8:16-18**

The purpose for John receiving this vision of the multitude and recording it is to continually provide hope for our Christian brothers and sisters who will experience great difficulties during this approaching time of great tribulation.

- It is intended to encourage them in their sufferings knowing that it is not worthy to be compared with the eternal glory that awaits those who remain steadfast in their faith unto death.

"Blessed are those who are persecuted for righteousness' sake, for theirs is the kingdom of heaven. Blessed are you when others revile you and persecute you and utter all kinds of evil against you falsely on my account. Rejoice and be glad, for your reward is great in heaven, for so they persecuted the prophets who were before you." *Matthew 5:10-12*

(Slides # 30 - 31)

144,000 IS A REMNANT OF THE CHURCH - NOT THE WHOLE

Again, it is a special privilege for some believers, granted by the Lord Himself that they might suffer for the sake of Christ.

> Only let your manner of life be worthy of the gospel of Christ....... <u>standing firm in one spirit, with one mind striving side by side for the faith of the gospel</u>, and <u>not frightened in anything by your opponents.</u> This is a clear sign to them of their destruction, but of your salvation, and that from God. <u>For it has been granted to you that for the sake of Christ you should not only believe in him but also suffer for his sake,</u> *Philippians 1:27-29*

Key Points:

"Striving side by side" is perhaps, <u>witnessing</u> <u>two by two</u> proclaiming the gospel in the midst of evil darkness which has come upon the entire earth.

➢ This is publicly proclaiming Jesus Christ without fear of the enemy even though you are in the midst of severe persecution. Joy remains in the hearts of these warriors.

➢ They love Jesus Christ and they love others more than they value their own lives.

Now the 144,000 who have been sealed for the mission of discipleship during the great tribulation will be greatly challenged.

➢ As it was with the apostle Paul, tough, challenging times await this sealed army of Christ.

➢ Yet, wherever they go proclaiming His name in the midst of chaos, they will go in a powerful anointing that will greatly impact many peoples across the earth.[30]

➢ A great revival lies ahead, but contrary to much modern day teaching, **the greatest revival will come in the midst of the greatest tribulation.**

Notes:

_____
_____
_____
_____
_____

---

[30] John 14:12-14

(Slide # 32 - 34)

LEADERSHIP QUALITIES THAT IDENTIFY THE "144,000"

They are among those historical champions of God who were willing to lay down their lives for the gospel of the kingdom. They understand that they will be persecuted by the world, but it doesn't deter them.

- They are Christians who continually deny themselves and take up the cross daily and follow Christ.[31]

- They are His true disciples in the latter days that view chaos as the greatest opportunity for the light to shine in the midst of darkness.

- They are warriors that continue to rejoice in the midst of trials for they know that it is through the bootcamp in the wilderness that faith and purity of heart is greatly strengthened.

- Their military mindset understands that there is no victory without a battle and one is not equipped for battle without the training received in the bootcamp of life's tough challenges.[32]

They are those who deeply sigh and groan over the sinful abominations that are committed in the midst of the nations.

- They are being sealed like their brothers and sisters were prior to the destruction of Jerusalem in the days of Ezekiel.[33]

- Today, these are those in the Body of Christ who recognize the challenging times that are coming quickly and they can be frequently found strengthening their relationship with the Lord in their respective prayer closets.

- They are habitual intercessors who understand that in order for true faith to be exercised, one needs to let go of the world and lay hold of Heaven. They are the "watchmen" who are prophets in the Army of God.[34]

Many Christians may believe that this is not for them; but it is for all who will hear His voice and begin to spiritually prepare.

In summary, the 144,000 "servants of God" do not include the entire church, but are the firstfruits of His people, those anointed disciples of Jesus that walk with Him for 3 ½ years during His latter day's ministry.

- This ministry is addressed in greater detail in a subsequent session.

---

[31] Luke 9:23
[32] James 1:2-4
[33] Ezekiel 9:4
[34] Isaiah 21:6; Ezekiel 3:17

Notes:
_____
_____
_____
_____
_____
_____

(Slide # 35)

THE NEXT SESSION:

First Read: Revelation 8 – 10

TRUMPETS, NUKES, & A LITTLE BOOK

- Opening the 7th Seal
- The Dawning of the Day of the Lord
- The Blowing of the 1st Trumpet that Burns 1/3 of the Land
- The Blowing of the 2nd Trumpet that Burns 1/3 of the Oceans
- The Blowing of the 3rd Trumpet that Burns 1/3 of the Fresh Waters
- The Blowing of the 4th Trumpet that Darkens 1/3 of the Daylight
- The Blowing of the 5th & 6th Trumpets & their Effect on 1/3 of Mankind

An Interlude:

- A Mighty Angel Descends with a "Little Book"

Additional Notes:
_____
_____
_____
_____
_____

THE LAMB OF GOD - OUR TRUE "COMMANDER-IN-CHIEF"

The days are rapidly approaching when a tremendous separation will take place among mankind.

Yet, during this present era of warfare, He reigns as our Commander-in-Chief and His Name continues to be the battle cry for those warriors who fight daily for righteousness and truth.

His name is Jesus, Our Lord, Our King, Our Commander-in-Chief

➢ A truly mighty Leader who would never delegate assignments to His people that He Himself wouldn't readily embrace.

➢ A Commander that Christian warriors will readily follow not matter the danger or what costs have to be paid.

➢ These are warriors whose deepest desire is to hear Jesus welcome them with the following words when they enter into His presence:

.... 'Well done, good and faithful servant. You have been faithful over a little; I will set you over much. Enter into the joy of your master.' *Matthew 25:21*

MINISTRY and RESOURCES

To arrange for speaking engagements with Dr. Don Bell use the following contact information:
    Email: Dr.Don.Bell@mcgmin.com
    Review Dr. Bell's profile at: www.mcgmin.com/authors.html
    Call: (888) 575-9626

This workbook, Keep What is Written, follows Dr. Bell's lesson series available on www.equippingwatchmen.com. This important lesson series is based on the following book:

God's Anointed Warriors
By Dr. Donald Bell (available now.)

    This book brings 21st century clarity to prophetic events recorded in the book of Revelation and the Lord's calling for warrior-spirited Christians of this generation.

    We are right on the verge of devastating events that will create great fear and chaos throughout the world and especially in our increasingly immoral and comfort-seeking nation.

    The reader is encouraged to follow Dr. Donald Bell in his in-depth study of Scripture that will bring greater clarity to numerous end-time events recorded in the Book of Revelation -events which are currently unfolding before our very eyes.

ISBN 978-1-943412-08-2

Published by -
Wilderness Voice Publishing
Canon City, Colorado USA
www.wvpbooks.com

This valuable resource can be obtained by the following:
- Amazon.com - Search: God's Anointed Warriors By Dr. Donald Bell
- Order from your local bookstore: ISBN 978-1-943412-08-2
- Wilderness Voice Publishing: http://wvpbooks-com.3dcartstores.com

www.ingramcontent.com/pod-product-compliance
Lightning Source LLC
Chambersburg PA
CBHW081015040426
42444CB00014B/3221